RABBIS

THE MANY FACES OF JUDAISM

ABOVE: Rabbi Chaskiel Chanin; OVERLEAF: Rabbi Dovber Malachowski with his son
Universe editor: Ellen R. Cohen; Writer: Michael Kress; Design by Milton Glaser, Inc.
A rabbi's appearance in this book does not necessarily constitute his or her approval of
an agreement with the beliefs, practices, customs, and opinions of the other rabbis in this book.
First published in the United States of America in 2002 by Universe Publishing
A Division of Rizzoli International Publications, Inc., 300 Park Avenue South, New York, NY 10010
2002 2003 2004 2005 2006 / 10 9 8 7 6 5 4 3 2 1

RABBIS
THE MANY FACES OF JUDAISM

GEORGE KALINSKY
100 UNEXPECTED PHOTOGRAPHS OF RABBIS
WITH ESSAYS IN THEIR OWN WORDS

Introduction by Senator Joe Lieberman
Foreword by Kirk Douglas

Universe

To June

And the rabbis said to me,
"The gates will open again,
and You will be blessed
with an angel."

ACKNOWLEDGMENTS
by George Kalinsky

There are many people I would like to thank. Most importantly I am indebted to the many rabbis who were gracious enough to find the time and commitment to write about special experiences in their lives. Each and every rabbi made this book a reality as they kindly let me into their world, for a little while.

In a book about Jewish leaders and teachers, I am proud and honored—as an American and as a Jew—to have Senator Joseph Lieberman write the introduction to my book.

I would like to express my heartfelt gratitude to Kirk Douglas, who never hesitated in his support. He has written a foreword with a spiritual elegance that is rarely achieved.

I feel particularly fortunate to have the enthusiasm of my publisher Charles Miers. My appreciation to my agent Jennifer Unter for her support, to Ezra Fitz for his research, and to Ellen Cohen, who spent endless hours of committed editing.

A special thanks to editor Michael Kress, who spent much time putting up with me while exhibiting his great skills and resources.

I am grateful to designer Milton Glaser and Wendy Gross for their encouragement and commitment to excellence. To my friend for many years, Rabbi Martin Rozenberg, who has shared the joys and tears with treasured support. And to Rabbi Shalom Paltiel, who is warm, bright, efficient, and wise beyond his years, and whose words always bring comfort.

My thanks to Dick Solomon and Charles Diker, for their support and guidance.

To the memory of Alexander Schindler, who inspired us "forever."

To my wonderful family, Emily and Jason, Lee and Michelle, Rachelle and Larry, Jonathan and Amy, Rhonit and Sadye.

This page would not be complete without acknowledging my adoring wife June who accompanied me through each phase of the book with understanding, intelligence, and charm.

INTRODUCTION
by Senator Joe Lieberman

We live in a time when the rabbinate is more diverse than ever. This book richly details that diversity through wonderful photographic portraits by George Kalinsky. These insightful self-portraits are by rabbis who have devoted their lives to sustaining and reviving the Jewish people. The powerful photographs bring the words of the rabbis to life, capturing the cultural richness that defines the Jewish people as a whole.

Beneath the differences lies an even more profound unity that manifests itself in a commitment to hold on to tradition, to make it relevant to a new generation of Jews, and to see purpose in the ongoing unfolding of history. By juxtaposing these rabbinic pictures and voices in one volume, Kalinsky has emphasized that which is common among the rabbis even as we are all aware of the differences that divide them. We often speak about pluralism and the importance of maintaining civil and respectful discourse in the face of disagreement. On September 11 we confronted a fundamentalism that justifies the killing of innocent people because of certainty about its own truth against that of others. More than ever, we need a religious model that can provide direction, shatter complacency, and emphasize the power of good, even as it displays the humility of knowing no one can have a monopoly on truth.

The heroes of this volume are men and women who wake up every morning trying to communicate those lessons to the communities in which they live, work, write, and preach. Perhaps the greatest tribute this book pays to them is to link their efforts to colleagues around the world who are doing the same thing. Together, they help inspire and direct us all.

FOREWORD
by Kirk Douglas

Sometimes I like to joke that I know more rabbis than Jews. After my first bar mitzvah, I lost religion, and religion lost me. But following the survival of a mid-air collision that resulted in the deaths of two young men, I began to study Torah with Rabbi Aaron in Jerusalem. Back home, in Los Angeles, I began to study with Rabbi Nachum Braverman and Rabbi David Wolpe following a debilitating stroke. I still study weekly with Rabbi Wolpe.

While my Judaic studies have not stirred me to become a more observant Jew, my knowledge has increased, and I have an increasingly rich spiritual life. Judaism has given me the desire to look for meaning in the midst of suffering, and has taught me to laugh with ever more abandon; both a result of a deeper and more abiding faith in God. My rabbis have taught me, through the use of classic texts, the answers and the questions to the most essential things in life: who am I, where do I come from, where am I going, what matters most?

Rabbis come in all shapes, sizes, and colors. George Kalinsky has captured them all. Here they are together: reconstructionist, reform, conservative, orthodox, and ultra-orthodox. They come from all over the world. They are all Jews. They are all teachers. They are all Israel.

Look at them. They are…tradition.

PREFACE
by George Kalinsky

As our taxi glided towards Jerusalem, one thing was sure: these hills were definitely not alive with the sound of music. Instead, the air was filled with a quiet aura of tension heightened by magnificent shards of sunlight. Conspicuously absent was the cacophony of pre-Shabbat traffic, impatient horns and irate drivers. In its place was an unnatural and foreboding silence. The sidewalks and bus stops were almost deserted. This was the day after a massacre of innocent teenagers in a discotheque bombing.

The taxi ride to the hotel in Jerusalem was over, and my journey to do a book on Rabbis had begun.

On the first night in our hotel, my wife June and I heard demonstrations and more terrorist bombings. We were warned not to go out, so we decided to stay in our hotel for dinner. We went down to the lavish lobby to discover we were alone, save for a piano player (perhaps named Sam) rendering *As Time Goes By* on a white baby grand. It was very eerie.

For the next several days I photographed some twenty Rabbis. Although there was quite a tension in the air, I felt that I was on a spiritual mission to put together a book that had never been done before.

I thought back to my days as a youngster growing up on Long Island, I can vividly remember our Rabbi being the focal point of our community. He was everywhere. He shared in our joyous events, inspired us with blessings, and was there to be a source of comfort during times of sorrow. But most of all, our Rabbi was our teacher. Rabbis seemed to have all the answers.

Going to our conservative synagogue on Shabbos was enjoyable for me because I always sat with my grandfather, Benjamin Rosen, whom I loved dearly. He was my first best friend. My earliest memories of that time period were the terrible reports of World War II, seeing alarming pictures of fighting, brutality, and the cruelty of war. So it was very comforting to me when "grandpa" kindly held my hand, offering me a sense of safety in the synagogue as we listened to the Rabbi's sermon. It gave me unique insight into the secular world and a spiritual perspective on the many questions that I had been formulating each week in anticipation of the Shabbos sermon.

Many years later, I visited New York City's Lower East Side to see the neighborhood my father Samuel had grown up in. He'd told me so many stories about how he struggled after the depression when his family "did not have what to eat."

I walked down Essex Street and and found myself wandering into a store selling religious artifacts. In the back of this spiritually cluttered establishment I saw a scribe, feather quill in hand, making final "repairs" to a Torah. I was struck by a moment of spiritual awe as the scribe, Rabbi Moshe Eisenbach, graciously gave me permission to photograph him as he performed the three thousand year old sacred task.

I had never witnessed such a thing before. As Rabbi Eisenbach's skilled hands danced over the parchment, I felt a direct connection to the history and traditions of Judaism, to the very Torah that Moses received at Mount Sinai thousands of years before.

It was then, as I gazed through my lens at Moses Eisenbach of Essex Street, that I knew I would do a book on Rabbis.

I started putting this book together in the spring of 2001. June and I were scheduling appointments in Paris when we got a call from Rabbi Yossi Gorodetzky urging us to meet the chief Rabbi of Israel, Meir Lau. We met him that evening at a fundraiser, along with Rabbi Pinto of France. They were both very gracious about my project and allowed me to photograph them.

THE NEXT MORNING WE WENT UP TO THE steps of Sacre Coeur to view the spectacular panorama of Paris. As I reached for my camera I felt a sudden twinge of panic. It wasn't there! It had been stolen, along with the film of Rabbis Lau and Pinto. At first I felt helpless and angry, but then I thought that perhaps those pictures were not meant to be taken. I looked over at June and smiled. We were together and unharmed. We held hands and walked away. Perhaps fate had employed this painful means of achieving its goal.

Since September 11, many of the Rabbis I have met have called me from all over the world, informing me of the worsening anti-Semitism that they were encountering. From France, Rabbi Gorodetzky told of terrorist bombings and the burning of a synagogue, and of being spit on as he walked down the street. From Rome, Rabbi Toaff, who presides over one of the most beautiful synagogues in the world, has to pass by soldiers with machine guns surrounding this sacred edifice twenty-four hours a day. From Barcelona, Rabbi Liebersohm wrote of the difficulties of being a Jew in Spain today. His words reminded me of having walked down the narrow, stone-lined streets of the old Jewish ghetto in Barcelona and realizing that some of the stones were actually Jewish gravestones desecrated during the Spanish Inquisition. To be a Jew in Spain has never been easy.

This reminded me of the Moscow Synagogue in 1988, where I observed a huge arena, spirituality enhanced with historical beauty. It was where my grandparents and great-grandparents had worshipped.

I wandered into a small study with Rabbi Martin Rozenberg and saw a man faintly visible in the shadows behind what appeared to be a rabbi concentrating at his desk. I was warned that this "evil in the shadows" was a KGB agent "on patrol" and that I should be very cautious. I took a tiny camera out of my pocket, snapped one quick photo from waist level, and then tucked the camera back away in a single motion. At the risk of being caught by the KGB and

possibly even jailed, I felt that I had to take this photo to show how lucky we were to live in a land of freedom. At the time I took this image, worshiping in the Soviet Union was frowned upon and many Jews caught observing their religion were beaten and sent to Siberia to do hard labor.

That moment propelled me into thinking about my freedom and how privileged we are to make choices. As Jews in the free world, we may observe our religious convictions as we wish. We are free to worship as Orthodox, Conservative, Reform, Reconstructionist, or Renewal. However, in compiling this book of Rabbis, I was surprised to find the degree of contention that exists among some rabbis of differing religious convictions.

We are at a precarious time in history. Our world is in a state of unrest, and terrorism and anti-Semitism are on the rise all over the world. We pray for world peace, pray that all men and women can live together in harmony. The Rabbis depicted here, though of differing denominations, form a unity by virtue of appearing in one book. May this unity find itself reflected in all Jews.

WHILE PHOTOGRAPHING RABBI TUVIA Bolton In Israel with the sounds of war in the background, I mentioned that I might not be quite as observant as I could be, but that I still put on the straps of the tefilin every morning. Rabbi Bolton maintained that we were both "men of faith" *(ba'al emunah)* and that all Jews stood at Sinai as one.

It is in that unified spirit that this book aims to portray Rabbis. To show them as the multi-faceted people that they are: leaders, teachers, preachers, scholars, spiritual innovators, chaplains, as well as fathers, mothers, avid hobbyists and professionals. Their portraits and words reveal men and women dedicated to their religion, their communities, their families, and themselves as human beings. In a word: Rabbis.

BOB ALPER
Comedian

Rabbi Alper, the world's most well-known practicing clergyman doing stand-up comedy–intentionally–performs throughout the U.S. and England, from the Hollywood Improv to synagogues, churches, theaters, and conventions. He is the author of two books and two comedy CDs, and lives in rural Vermont with his wife.

"When my turn came, I walked onto the comedy club stage wearing a pulpit robe (but not a tallit), spread my arms as wide as I could, and intoned, 'Try not to think of me…as a rabbi.' The crowd howled."

M y business card reads: Dr. Robert A. Alper, Rabbi/Stand-Up Comic (Really). The "(Really)" isn't just a way to be cute. It serves an important purpose. A few years ago, while flying out of Omaha, I found myself sitting across the aisle from former Senator Bob Kerry. At one point, just to pass the time while the meal was being served, he turned to me and said, "So, what do you do?"

"I'm a rabbi and a stand-up comic."

"Really?"

I offered him my card.

While attending my thirtieth high school reunion, an old classmate reminded me of something I'd long forgotten: as a teenager, I apparently amused my friends by telling them that I wanted to be a rabbi and a comedian.

The improbable combination originated during New England regional conferences of Reform Judaism's National Federation of Temple Youth. It's talent night, and Bobby Alper shyly takes the stage. He performs an adapted version of a Shelley Berman or Bob Newhart comedy routine. The audience laughs. Bobby becomes a popular guy, is elected to various high offices, and best of all, the girls pay attention. Comedy is good.

With a childhood centered on our Reform synagogue and with my uncle, a rabbi, as a role model, the rabbinate was a natural career path, while comedy never even entered the equation. Except it was always there, through the preppy Lehigh University period and the earnest seminary years. Hebrew Union College's most intimidating moment came during the fourth year, when each student must deliver a sermon before students and faculty, followed by a critique. When my turn arrived, I stood nervously behind the lectern, gripping the velvet overlay made black by the perspiration of generations of student rabbis. I began with the same drone that echoed through that chapel week after week. But after about ninety seconds, from out of the ceiling speaker, a female voice interrupted me. "That's boring!" she said.

For the remainder of the sermon we engaged in a dialogue–all scripted, of course–with a few terrific laughs and a serious message at the

conclusion. That year, I won the prize for sermon delivery and oratory. Comedy is good.

For fourteen years I occupied pulpits, six years as an assistant rabbi in a 1,600-family congregation in Buffalo, and eight as rabbi of a 450-family congregation outside Philadelphia. I earned a doctorate along the way, and in 1986 decided to leave congregational life and begin a counseling practice, sharing office space with a psychiatrist. But that same summer, Philadelphia's Jewish Exponent ran a small ad soliciting entrants for the first annual "Jewish Comic of the Year Contest." Irresistible.

When my turn came, I walked onto the comedy club stage wearing a pulpit robe (but not a tallit), spread my arms as wide as I could, and intoned, "Try not to think of me…as a rabbi." The crowd howled. I came in third, behind a chiropractor and a lawyer, but one of the judges, host of the area's top-rated morning TV show, loved my routine and invited me to appear on her program. A new career was born.

By 1990, I was doing comedy full time but still had time to write an inspirational book, *Life Doesn't Get Any Better Than This*. I continue to conduct High Holiday services near Philadelphia, and very occasionally officiate at a wedding or a funeral. But week in and week out, I make people laugh. And frequently, when the laugh is a sustained one and I can take a quick breather, I think with amazement, "This is my 'job!'" What a job.

There has always been a lot of comedy in my rabbinate. My guiding principle: When you hear them laughing, you know they're listening. Sermons, lectures, counseling, weddings, and even funerals, where appropriate, include humor. Not a full routine, not a knee-slapping laugh fest, but enough to engage and relax the listeners. Then the serious message to follow can be delivered much more effectively.

Conversely, there has always been a lot of rabbi in my comedy. Not just the topics, but the type of humor I use. Absolutely clean and unhurtful, with nothing racist, homophobic, sexist, or the like. The comment I cherish most after all these years? As an elderly man left a show, he whispered to me, "Thank you for respecting us."

MARC ANGEL

Congregation Shearith Israel, the Spanish and Portuguese Synagogue, New York City

Rabbi Angel is the former president of the Rabbinical Council of America. He is the rabbi of Congregation Shearith Israel, in New York City, which was founded in 1654.

"I never saw or ate chopped liver, gefilte fish, cholent, or kugel until I enrolled as a student in Yeshiva College in the fall of 1963. When these foods were served on my first Shabbat at Yeshiva, I asked class-mates what they were. They looked at me incredulously: Was I really Jewish?"

Excerpted and adapted with permission of the author from But Who Am I and Who Are My People: A Rabbi's Reflec-tions on the Rabbinate and the Jewish Com-munity, *by Rabbi Marc D. Angel (Ktav Publishing House, 2001).*

G rowing up as a Sephardic Jew–someone from Spanish or Middle Eastern descent–I learned quickly that the dominant Ashkenazic (East European-derived) community had little knowledge or concern with Sephardic culture. In the Jewish day school of Seattle, where I grew up, we learned Jewish customs and tradi-tions almost exclusively from an Ashkenazic point of view. Sephardic history, rituals, holiday obser-vance, foods, music, intellectual life–all were consistently ignored. It was as though Sephardim had no past and no civilization worth discussing. I don't believe the teachers taught this way from malice, but simply from ignorance. The Sephardic tradition was of no interest to them.…

I never saw or ate chopped liver, gefilte fish, cholent, or kugel until I enrolled as a student in Yeshiva College in the fall of 1963. When these foods were served on my first Shabbat at Yeshiva, I asked classmates what they were. They looked at me incredulously: Was I really Jewish? How was it possible for a Jew, let alone a religious Jew, not to know what these basic Sabbath foods were? I explained to them that I was Sephardic and that we ate different foods in honor of the Sabbath. They could hardly believe this.

A number of my Yiddish-speaking teachers consistently referred to me as Engel. Angel, a fine Sephardic name, did not sound Jewish to them, whereas Engel, a fine Ashkenazic name, did. Most Judaic studies teachers taught laws and customs exclusively from the Ashkenazic perspective. (Yeshiva did institute a Sephardic program under the leadership of Haham Solomon Gaon, thereby making it possible for students to become somewhat familiar with Sephardic *halakhic*–legal–positions.) A number of people, upon learning I was Sephardic, commented that they thought Sephardic life had come to an end with the expulsion of Jews from Spain in 1492. That Sephardim had continued to flourish throughout the Ottoman Empire, the Middle East, North Africa, and Western Europe seems not to have made an indentation in their con-sciousness. That Sephardim had been the pioneers of Jewish life in the New World also went unno-ticed and unappreciated.

Much of my career as a Sephardic rabbi has been devoted to studying and teaching about the Sephardic experience. My goal has been to inculcate Sephardic traditions among Sephardim, as well as to make the larger Ashkenazic community aware of the Sephardic component of the Jewish people.

In September 1969, I began serving Congregation Shearith Israel, the historic Spanish and Portuguese Synagogue in New York City, which was founded in 1654. I sat on the *tebah* (reader's desk) next to the rabbi emeritus, Dr. David de Sola Pool, and across from Dr. Louis C. Gerstein, rabbi, and the Rev. A. Lopes Cardozo, *hazzan* (cantor). I have been sitting in that same seat now for thirty years. My wife, Gilda, and I have watched our own family grow. Our son, Hayyim, who was born the month after I began service at Shearith Israel, now sits next to me on the tebah as associate rabbi of Shearith Israel. I have now participated in the life of the congregation on a daily basis for all these years. I have known three, four, and in some cases, five generations of families associated with Shearith Israel. The congregation has been our extended family.

In the fall of 1978, I continued my work to spread knowledge of the Sephardic world by founding Sephardic House, with the encourage-ment of several Sephardic laymen. It was based in Shearith Israel under my leadership. As it grew into a national organization, Sephardic House moved into its own offices, though I have contin-ued to serve actively as honorary president. Sephardic House has been active in promoting Sephardic culture through classes, lectures, film festivals, concerts, and publications. It has become an important cultural resource and center for information about Sephardic life.

One of the basic responsibilities of rabbis is to nourish a spirit of unity and understanding within a Jewish community that is diverse and segmented. Good rabbis lose sleep trying to cope with this duty.

MORDECHAI SHMUEL ASHKENAZI

Chief Rabbi, Kfar Chabad of Israel

Author of five books, Rabbi Ashkenazi is Chief Rabbi of Kfar Chabad, the Israeli town that is haven and home to Israel's Lubavitch Hassidim, and which contains an exact replica of the Rebbe's Brooklyn home.

"One of my main goals in life is to encourage young Chabad Hasidim to become practicing rabbis. I also always strive to aid fellow rabbis who have difficulties or questions."

I began my role as *rav* of Kfar Chabad– the Israeli town populated by Chabad-Lubavitch Hasidim–in 1973. I strive to be the guardian of the Kfar, and I do all I can to assure that it remains what the Rebbe wanted it to be: a Chabad community that brings blessings and joy to all of Israel.

One of my main goals in life is to encourage young Chabad Hasidim to become practicing rabbis. I also always strive to aid fellow rabbis who have difficulties or questions.

My whole purpose in life is to carry out the directions of the Lubavitch Rebbe. I believe that the Rebbe is Messiah and that through following his ideas we will improve the entire world. In fact, I believe the Rebbe is the only Jewish leader who even thought in those terms. I therefore take my role as Chief Rabbi of Kfar Chabad, the center of Chabad in Israel–which itself is the center of the world–extremely seriously.

But it isn't easy. We as Chabad members, are not generally involved in politics, but we often find it impossible to sit on the sidelines. When former Prime Minister Benjamin Netanyahu went against the wishes of the Rebbe and made agreements with the Palestinians at Wye, I was forced to become of one of the first to protest publicly, and I continued my outcry until Netanyahu finally fell, losing his re-election bid.

I have also done much work in Russia. All of the Chabad houses in Russia that have built *mikvahs*–ritual baths–have done so under my supervision. Similarly, I have presided over hundreds of conversions in Russia to make sure that they are according to the laws of the Torah.

But for the last five years I have concentrated on a new project that the Rebbe gave me many years ago but which I had been too busy to truly devote much time to until recently. I am writing a massive work that will certainly fill many books: a commentary on the unique compendium of Jewish law called *Shulchan Aruch HaRav*, written by Rabbi Shneur Zalman of Liadi, the first leader of the Chabad Hasidim, some 200 years ago.

RAHAMIM BANIN
Director, Chabad of Venice

Rabbi Banin is Chief Chabad Rabbi of Venice. He established the first and only kosher restaurant in Venice located at the entrance of the world's oldest Jewish ghetto—traced to the year 1516–on the Cannaregio Canal. Rabbi Banin is also director of the first rabbinical yeshiva in Venice in 200 years.

"It is my hope to continue to establish Venice as a community where the observance and dissemination of the vital institutions of Jewish life take place."

C habad of Venice has been dedicated to the revival of the Jewish Ghetto in Venice, the oldest-known Jewish Ghetto in the world. During the fifteenth, sixteenth, and seventeenth centuries, Venice and its Jewish community was of primary importance, as it served as the world's major printer of *seforim*, Jewish texts. Now, each year, approximately ten thousand Jews spend Shabbos, the Sabbath, with us, visit GAM-GAM restaurant for a kosher meal, or just stop in the yeshiva or Chabad House–our headquarters and synagogue–to say hello.

Recently, in the daily Venetian newspaper, *Il Gazzettino*, Chabad of Venice was recognized as the only thriving source of Jewish life in Venice, which has continued to grow; while prior to our arrival ten years ago, the Jewish life and population dwindled.

Along with my wife, Shachar, our endeavors to further develop the community also include active involvement with Venetians through providing the daily *minyanim*–prayer services–for the city, weekly outreach programs, special events during the Jewish holidays, a campaign for a kosher *mikve*–ritual bath–and a future *cheder*, academy for youngsters. These efforts have attracted new families who have made Venice their permanent home.

At the Chabad House, which serves as a welcoming center to the Ghetto, we are available to answer questions, distribute information or just to offer cold drinks and snacks to travelers. An innumerable number of Jews of all ages have actually had their Bar-Mitzvahs, putting on tefillin for the first time in their lives with us.

Another successful project, which has become one of Venice's Jewish highlights, is GAM-GAM Kosher Restaurant. GAM-GAM becomes the light and life of the Ghetto, with its world-renowned Shabbos hospitality program, overflowing with singing, dancing, and words of Torah–not to mention great food–for the hundreds of guests who visit us every week, from the four corners of the globe.

The original idea for Venice's first and only kosher restaurant was not only to appeal to one's appetite. GAM-GAM has become a special gathering place for Venetians and travelers alike, catering to a myriad of tastes with its inviting atmosphere and diverse cuisine, while supporting its original goal of bringing life back into the Ghetto. By simply enjoying a meal at GAM-GAM, people actually become an important part of history: the history of the revitalization of Jewish life in the world's oldest ghetto. GAM-GAM was opened with the intent that it should be a Jewish oasis to assist the kosher traveler and to encourage those not-yet-kosher.

In addition to kosher food, every city needs to have a yeshiva, as Torah learning is a key to Jewish survival. In our yeshiva and learning center, young men receive rabbinic ordination and travelers and community members come in for classes or individual learning. The friendly and engaging environment of the Yeshiva of Venice demonstrates to Jews that we live in a unique time when anyone can afford to spend some part of their day learning about Yiddishkeit, whether it be for fifteen minutes or five hours.

Another vital key to Jewish survival is *Taharas Hamishpocha*, family purity. After a few years of effort to raise the money, we recently acquired a small property and building worth $90,000, convenient to the Ghetto, yet privately located. We are now working hard to raise the remaining $110,000 required for the actual construction of the mikve, which we are hoping to be able to start building soon. If there was only one woman who needed the mikve here in Venice, this, in itself, would justify its construction. But we receive countless calls and e-mails every week from travelers asking for assistance in coordinating mikve plans, proving the importance of this major project.

It is my hope to continue to establish Venice as a community where the observance and dissemination of the vital institutions of Jewish life take place. Hashem (G-d) has provided each and every Jew with the capacity to carry out the mitzvos in daily life in the fullest measure, for otherwise, it would not be logical or fair of G-d to give obligations and duties which are impossible to fulfill.

JEFF BEARMAN
Licensed Israel Tour Guide

Rabbi Bearman is a rabbi who made aliyah (immigration to Israel) after growing up and being educated at Reform and Conservative schools in the states. In addition to being a licensed tour guide in Israel, Bearman is a bar and bat mitzvah officiant.

"A rabbi is a teacher, and in my work both as a guide and officiant I attempt to help the people I meet to understand the dynamics which make Israel the perplexing, contradictory, interesting, fascinating, and creative country that it is."

After seven years in the rabbinate in the United States, I made aliyah to Israel in 1979, where I now work as a licensed Israel tour guide and officiant at the bar and bat mitzvah ceremonies of visitors from abroad. A rabbi is a teacher, and in my work both as a guide and officiant I attempt to help the people I meet to understand the dynamics which make Israel the perplexing, contradictory, interesting, fascinating, and creative country that it is.

Like life in general, the modern state of Israel is full of paradoxes. It is the story of a people reborn, both on a communal and individual basis. On the tombstone of David Ben Gurion, Israel's first prime minister, in the town of Sde Boker, three dates are listed: his birthdate, the date of his arrival in the Land of Israel, and the date of his death. Ben Gurion was of the opinion that the day he got off the boat and touched the holy soil of the Holy Land marked the beginning of a new state of existence in his life. He had not really lived until he made aliyah. After a few years of getting acclimated to my new home, I too feel that my life began anew when I got off the EL AL 747 jetliner at Ben Gurion Airport. As the Hebrew expression goes, I came to Israel to build and to be built. In spite of the numerous ups and downs I have experienced on a personal and communal level, there is no doubt that for myself I made the correct choice.

It is a long way from St. Paul, Minnesota, to Jerusalem, Israel. Like all Jewish kids my age, I went to Hebrew School three days a week. Most of the children hated it, but somewhere along the line the dynamic spirit of Jewish life and culture grabbed my attention.

As a young teenager, I visited Israel for the first time in 1959. I remember that there were six of us from the Temple of Aaron, and we brought a Torah scroll that we donated to a school in the Israeli city of Ashkelon. I received two degrees, one from Columbia University and the other from the Jewish Theological Seminary. Though my anthropology major at Columbia interested me, it was my Judaic studies at JTS that really got my attention. I spent my fourth year of the five-year program in Jerusalem, at the Haim Greenberg Institute and Hebrew University. While there, I met the woman I would later marry, Susie, from Buenos Aires. I was ordained at Hebrew Union College, and during my studies there I spent a year in Jerusalem.

Upon being ordained I served as a congregational rabbi in Fargo, North Dakota; East Windsor, New Jersey; and as a United States Air Force chaplain at Scott Air Force Base, Illinois. My original goal in becoming a rabbi was to be of service to the Jewish community; in particular I always enjoyed leading worship services.

My forte as a pulpit rabbi was adult education and lifecycle events. Now, as a guide and bar/bat mitzvah officiant I am able to continue doing what I do best. Many years ago I officiated for a young girl who did not want to be bat mitzvah. When we arrived at Masada—the ancient Jewish fortress remains—from Jerusalem, she simply did not want to go through with the ceremony. I was riding along with the family and could feel the tension oozing out between the teenager and her parents. Not wanting to force my will on anybody, I suggested we just forget the ceremony for the moment, and promised that I would come by that evening to have a chat with the family, whom I had just met a day or two previously in preparation for the ceremony. Although my pastoral counseling skills were somewhat rusty since I had arrived in Israel and ceased working for a synagogue, I must have done something right, because two days later I held a Shabbat afternoon bat mitzvah service for the family, which went quite well. One important lesson I learned from the incident: Roll with the waves. Don't force anything, because it does not work.

My life has changed immensely since those early days in Minnesota. At the time, I never would have dreamed that I would be living my life, doing my work, and raising a family in the ancient-yet-modern homeland of the Jewish people. The first sabra—native-born Israeli—in my family is my granddaughter, Rotem. May she be the first of many more Bearman sabras to be born in this land of mystery and enchantment.

JOE BLACK
Congregation Albert, Albuquerque, N.M.

Rabbi Black is the recording artist for "Leave a Little Bit Undone," "Aleph Bet Boogie," and other Jewish music releases.

"For me, when I write, play, or just listen to music, I am transported to another level, and it brings me closer to God."

My son Ethan was born on Rosh Hashanah, eight years ago. It was the first time I was not in synagogue on the Jewish New Year in more than thirty years. That experience made me so aware of the wonder of being in God's presence: A new life came into the world on the day the world was created. I never hesitated in my decision to be at the hospital, rather than synagogue, on that day. All rabbis must juggle multiple lives: We are spouses, teachers, employees, public figures, and parents. All rabbis must struggle with the dilemmas that those often-competing roles pose, because the rabbinate is a calling that is extraordinarily demanding.

I've always had duel fascinations with Judaism and music. Growing up in Chicago, I was very active in Jewish youth movements there, taught Hebrew school and music, and was a cantorial soloist at several synagogues. While at college at Northwestern I played in various clubs, and then I was chosen to be the host of a TV program in Chicago called *The Magic Door*, which was a well-known Jewish children's show. We won an Emmy my last year on the show.

After my sophomore year at Northwestern, I took some time off from school to decide whether I wanted to pursue a career in music or the Rabbinate. During that year, I worked as a cantorial soloist and song leader. I also did my television show. After a while, however, I realized that I missed the intellectual and spiritual components of studying Torah and involving myself fully in Jewish life—not merely as a performer. It was at that point that I decided to apply to rabbinical school. I was accepted at Hebrew Union College and spent my first year in Jerusalem.

Being a rabbi and a teacher calls for me to use whatever skills I have, and my music is a big piece of that. Music is a gift that God gives us; I have been blessed with certain talents and skills. I do not know where they come from, so there is something holy about them. For me, when I write, play, or just listen to music, I am transported to another level, and it brings me closer to God.

I could never be a professional musician exclusively; doing so would be feeding my belly but not my soul. My rabbinate is more important to me than my music. My music does not define my rabbinate, my rabbinate defines my music.

I have never wanted to be known as "the singing rabbi," so I did not even pick up my guitar during my first year in Minneapolis, where I served as Assistant—and later, Associate Rabbi—at Temple Israel, right out of rabbinical school. That changed when the nursery school asked if I would do a fundraising concert, which I did. It was well received, and the following year, they asked if I would do a recording for them, so I started writing music. Some members of the congregation, who were involved in the music industry, suggested I use that cassette to develop and release an album, and that is how my professional recording career began.

After nine years in Minneapolis, I was ready to lead my own congregation and wanted a more intimate setting. I ended up in New Mexico, where I have remained until today. My congregants understand who I am, they celebrate my music, they celebrate my rabbinate, and I celebrate the congregation. It is a great fit for me.

Being a rabbi gives me an opportunity to make a difference in the lives of individuals, my congregation, and the community at large. New Mexico does not have a large Jewish community, and as the rabbi of the largest synagogue in the state, I have a unique role that I take very seriously. I can speak out on public issues, and I have the ear of many people. I serve on the boards of many community organizations. I am involved in the state's anti–death penalty movement, the Martin Luther King Multicultural Council, and the New Mexico Symphony Orchestra; I meet with the governor and senators frequently, and I was among the clergy members picked to meet with the president when he visited the area. I will soon begin serving as a chaplain in the Albuquerque police department—the first Jewish chaplain in the city police. Being involved in the community and having a powerful voice is important to me. I do not take my pulpit for granted, and that role means a lot to me.

I have found my spiritual home here in Albuquerque and specifically at Congregation Albert. I can pray here—for that, I feel eternally blessed.

TUVIA BOLTON

Assistant Rosh Yeshiva (head of school), Ohr Tmimim in Kfar Chabad, Israel

Rabbi Bolton is the guitar-strumming head rabbi of Yeshiva Ohr Tmimim, a major academy in Kfar Chabad. Rabbi Bolton came to his current life via the University of Michigan and an entirely irreligious upbringing to find his spiritual and communal home among the Hassidim of Israel. He has recently returned to writing and performing music.

"About eight years ago the Rebbe made the seemingly simple statement: 'Do what you can to bring Moshiach [the Messiah].' It really struck a note in my brain, and I began to compose songs again, a pastime that had not interested me at all for twenty years."

It was the Sixties, and the spirit of those times, of course, was that everyone acted as if they were sure they were one hundred percent right about whatever insanity they believed in. The only semistable thing in those crazy days seemed to be rock 'n' roll music–and it saved me.

I had been brought up in a secular Jewish home in Detroit. I graduated from the University of Michigan in 1967 with a degree in philosophy. I considered law, medicine, and teaching, but my planning was stymied by existential problems that I was facing. In the end though, I drove a delivery truck by day to make money, and at night I sang in bars.

I clung to the music for dear life, and it got to the point that I was the lead singer in four different bands, each for a different type of crowd: soul, country, fraternity, and psychedelic; for black, hillbilly, frat, and hippie bars, respectively.

Meanwhile, I was searching for truth.

I went to a lecture of a certain Professor Timothy Leary when he visited the campus on a world tour. Besides being very charismatic, he made an anti-Semitic statement: "The only evil is the Theistic Jews and their jealous G-d." His statement inspired me to give up drugs and started me thinking that maybe Jews are special.

Around that time, people were getting interested in meditation and religion, often as a way of permanently replicating their drug experiences. I, too, became interested in religions and religious experiences. I read many big books and it all seemed the same: heaven, hell, "Follow me, I am the way." Sort of like *Alice in Wonderland*. So I canceled out of all that too.

It's a long story, but finally I figured I'd give Judaism a try.

I read the Bible in English and was baffled by the stories of Abraham, Isaac, and Jacob. These men seemed to be giants although they didn't really do anything. I also couldn't figure out the *korbonot* (animal sacrifices), which seemed very primitive and totally non-Jewish–and there they were, page after page of them, smack in the middle of the Good Book.

I went with my questions to a Reform, then a Conservative, rabbi and was really turned off by what seemed to me to be a lack of "soul." Then I read that some rabbi called Y. Kagen was giving lectures on Hassidic Judaism, so I went. Half a year later, I was sitting in a yeshiva for "late beginners" in Brooklyn, learning Torah.

Four years later I moved to Israel, and a year later got married to an Israeli girl. When I got a job teaching in another "late beginners" yeshiva called Ohr Tmimim in Kfar Chabad–a village not far from Tel Aviv–we moved there.

About eight years ago the Rebbe made the seemingly simple statement: "Do what you can to bring Moshiach [the Messiah]." It really struck a note in my brain, and I began to compose songs again, a pastime that had not interested me at all for twenty years. Since then, I have made two tapes and am in the middle of a third. I have been on national Israeli television four times. I began writing a weekly Torah essay, which is sent to about four thousand people every week by e-mail.

It has been twenty years since I moved to Kfar Chabad. I'm still at Ohr Tmimim, but now, thank G-d, with four children and one grandchild. May we all be dancing together with Moshiach–now!

BARUCH B. BORCHARDT

Executive Director, Agudath Israel of America

Rabbi Borchardt was born in Hamburg, Germany, and at the age of fourteen fled to Shanghai, China. There he joined the famed Mirer Yeshiva, which had moved to Shanghai when the clouds of World War II began to gather in Europe. After the war was over, he moved to the United States where, shortly thereafter, he joined the staff of Agudath Israel of America, which he currently serves as executive director.

"I feel my work as a rabbi is to help build the Jewish community into one where Torah is truly respected and fully embraced."

E veryone has a mission in the world and each of us has to learn what his mission is and for what purpose he was created by G-d.

After my parents tried their utmost to give me a good Jewish education and with the guidance of G-d I realized that my duty in the world is to serve Him to the best of my abilities.

And I realized my obligation involves doing what I can to help my fellow Jews in any way I can, without compromise.

A Jew is created by the Creator to spend all his life improving the World, and I feel my work as a rabbi is to help build the Jewish community into one where Torah is truly respected and fully embraced.

This is the mission of Agudath Israel, the organization I serve: to build and strengthen Torah throughout the world—Torah, in its entirety and without any compromise. We want to help Jews do their best to keep the Mitzvos (commandments) of the Torah, and we refuse to water down the Torah's ideals.

I see myself as a little wheel in a large effort to promote a strong, living Judaism that fully reflects the ideals of Torah.

Not everything is accomplished with big deeds. Assisting individual Jews when they need help or advice that my experience and background allow me to offer is how I see my role as a rabbi. I live for the hope that I can provide Torah knowledge and advice for helping solve day-to-day problems of other Jews, whether they have to do with theology, prayer, keeping kosher, Shabbos or any other area of a Jew's life.

That is my mission as a rabbi—but really it's my mission as a Jew.

EUGENE B. BOROWITZ

Sigmund L. Falk Distinguished Professor of Education and Jewish Religious Thought, Hebrew Union College-Jewish Institute of Religion

Rabbi Borowitz has authored fifteen volumes on Jewish theology and his new book is the most recent in the Jewish Publication Society's series, Scholar of Distinction. An anthology culled from fifty years of his shorter papers, it is entitled *Studies in the Meaning of Judaism.*

"My greatest challenge is to transform my classroom from the rigid, hierarchical one of my school years to one of inter-personal exchange, while not sacrificing the demands of Jewish learning."

Excerpted with permission from Judaism After Modernity: Papers from a Decade of Fruition, *by Eugene B. Borowitz (New York: University Press of America, 1999).*

Much of my Jewish religious life derives from an ambivalent impression of my Ohio childhood. I liked being Jewish. I even enjoyed religious school and going to services. But it exasperated me that my teachers and my rabbi could never explain Judaism in any way that made sense to me. When I discovered that philosophy and the social sciences were not any smarter, I decided to become a rabbi.

Then my ambivalence intensified. I loved the Hebrew Union College in theory, but only occasionally in practice. Once again, my teachers left me badly disappointed. Along with my two close friends, Arnie Wolf and Steve Schwarzschild, I figured I had better build my own sort of Jewish faith and find my own way of explaining it. And that is what I am still doing.

A consequent student experiment was critical. I was not worried about my intellectual life. That came easily to me. But making personal contact with God was strange to my American upbringing. So I decided to try to learn to pray, not just at the daily college service, but by myself. That way there would be no dodging God. Besides, I and some others of my classmates wanted to be more Jewish. We knew we were modern. What bothered us was how to be Jews....

As a rabbi, I struggle with many of the things that bother other rabbis. People do not seem to care very much about Judaism. Regardless of my best efforts, they do not take it seriously or find my understanding of it very compelling. Despite the occasional life I have touched and the faithful remnant who care, I often feel that, on the human level, my work does not really mean very much. It helps when I can remember that God will one day win out even without my success. I found it hard to acknowledge that I was not the Messiah, not even the bringer of the Messianic age. It is harder still remembering that I am not God.

My greatest spiritual shock has come from the intense loneliness I feel as a Jew. My ethical and cultural friends think religion odd. My Jewish companions, the few who are learned and serious, think Reform Judaism intolerably undemanding. I do have the rare good fortune to have Reform colleagues with whom I can discuss Jewish intellectual issues. But we go rather independent ways when it comes to understanding our Judaism, particularly should we ever talk of Jewish faith.

My sense of isolation is intensified by my strong commitment to the notion of Judaism as a community religion. Even desiring a rich Jewish ethnicity makes one an alien to much of American Jewish life. But if one wants to be a self and fulfill oneself in a Jewish community of selves, in Martin Buber's sense, then alienation becomes the common stuff of one's Jewish existence. In this respect, my experience differs from that of many colleagues. I have spent almost all my rabbinic years working on someone else's staff. I have not been able, therefore, like congregational rabbis, to take the leading role in shaping the community in which I function....

I have some partially effective strategies for alleviating my solitariness. I am blessed with a good marriage and children who still talk to me, and I work hard at keeping it that way. I have a few friends and enjoy a few pleasures. And I try to create community wherever I can. My greatest challenge is to transform my classroom from the rigid, hierarchical one of my school years to one of inter-personal exchange, while not sacrificing the demands of Jewish learning. That effort has also given me my greatest rewards. Furthermore, I have the joy of working with colleagues who agree that we must make a serious effort to have our school less an institution than a community. And from time to time, we and our students actually bring it into being.

Mostly, I have learned a new aspect of Jewish messianism. Of course, I hope for justice and look forward to peace. I still aspire to the ultimate vindication of the Jewish people, and through it, of all humanity. But now, too, I long for redemption from the *galut*–exile–of loneliness, for that day when we shall all be one as persons and one in community–for only on that day will God be in our lives as God, to God, is God.

SHMULEY BOTEACH

National Radio Host; author and lecturer

*"To this day I cannot
imagine that there is
a higher calling than
healing the soul and
mending of spirit."*

W hen I was eight years old, my parents divorced. My mother, my siblings, and I moved to Miami, while my father stayed in Los Angeles. I was not the first or the last child of a divorce to face this reality, but the prevalence of this phenomenon did not make it any easier for me.

My parents' divorce instigated within me a cynicism that grew to realize its full-grown shape around the time of my thirteenth birthday. I was not interested in school, for I had come to the cynical belief that nothing really mattered.

But an unexpected source of influence at the time was the Lubavitch organization, the world-wide Jewish education network. The Lubavitchers had an active branch in Miami, and I would ride my moped to South Beach, where the rabbinical college was located. There I would kibitz with the older rabbinical students whom I had met through the Lubavitch summer camp. One of them, Shneur Zalman Fellig, presented me with a very special gift on the occasion of my Bar Mitzvah: He invited me to join him on a trip to New York, where I would have the chance to meet with the leader of the Lubavitch movement, the great Rebbe, Rabbi Menachem Schneerson.

Before my trip, I wrote a letter to give the Rebbe when I met him. It spoke of the cynicism I felt clouding my soul as a result of my parents' divorce. I told him that I felt broken and I did not know how I would ever heal. We waited for hours through the night in a line to see the Rebbe. When it finally came to my turn, I stepped into the room where he sat, and handed him the letter. Shortly into the text he looked up from my carefully penned words with his piercing blue eyes. He spoke: "You are too young to be a cynic already. I bless you today to grow to be a great light, first to your family and your school, and then to all the Jewish people and all the world."

I left the room with a radiant glow and a lightness in my soul. Here was the foremost Jewish spiritual force in the world telling a cynical teenager that great things awaited him. It was the next morning, believe it or not, when I determined that the rabbinate was to be my calling.

I had also realized that life could, indeed, be imbued with purpose.

From there I took the practical steps needed in order to pursue the path that had so eloquently been revealed to me. I begged my mother to allow me to go away to rabbinical school. She was hesitant, but after a year of my badgering her with applications and forms, she helped me to apply to a Lubavitcher Yeshiva in Los Angeles.

And so, in my decision to become a rabbi, I sought to take my broken heart and wounded spirit and transform them into a life choice that would heal myself and others. Finally, the pain that I had experienced in my early years would be transformed into something that was healing and life-affirming. To this day I cannot imagine that there is a higher calling than healing the soul and mending of spirit.

And of course, my position as a rabbi affects all that I do. Since the publication of my book, *Kosher Sex,* I am often asked, "What exactly are you? A relationship guru? A sex expert?" In truth, I am neither. I am simply a rabbi, and everything else that I do emanates through that specific lens, like light through a prism. The multitudes of roles that then radiate from the other end of that prism are vast and varied. They are the roles of advisor, of marriage counselor, of listener, of teacher. I am a father, and a brother, and always a son. I am a writer and an observer of life.

Many feel that I strayed from my appropriate territory when I wrote *Kosher Sex,* for it dealt with subjects that were outside the rabbinic purview. In response, I point out that the Talmud itself includes discourse on every subject, from relationships to happiness to world issues to sexuality. It is not simply a guide for how we are to conduct the spiritual side of our life. Rather it is a guide that addresses each and every area of our life. It is a map for our very existence.

I have dedicated my life to dispelling the myth that G-d is present only in our designated holy places. On the contrary, G-d is everywhere. Our faith should therefore bleed into our "every-day" life. My faith affects everything I do, for it makes me who I am.

BALFOUR BRICKNER

Executive Director, The Alfred and Gail Engelberg Foundation;
Senior Rabbi Emeritus, Stephen Wise Free Synagogue

Rabbi Brickner
is a published
author of books,
pamphlets, journal
articles, film guides,
filmstrips, and
newspaper columns.
His books include
*Searching the
Prophets for Values*.
For seven years he
wrote and hosted
a national radio
program: "Advent-
ures in Judaism,"
winner of four
Ohio State Awards
for outstanding
religious broadcast-
ing. He appears
regularly on local
and national radio
and TV. He has two
grown sons and
two grandchildren.

*"The rabbinate, as
it turned out, is
probably the greatest
career for a person
who likes people and
who wants to make a
difference in society."*

"**H**e'll be a rabbi when the Messiah comes." Those were the words of my grandfather (may his memory be for a blessing) when he first heard I was attending the Hebrew Union College in Cincinnati, the seminary that trained men–and today, men and women–for the Reform rabbinate. I understood his sentiment perfectly. In fact, at the time, I probably agreed with him.

I had no intention of becoming a rabbi. I had grown up in a rabbinical home. My father, Barnett, may his memory be for a blessing, was the rabbi of a very large Reform Jewish congregation in Cleve-land and one of the giants of the American Reform rabbinate. My mother was a distinguished Jewish educator and one of the first women in New York City in the early 1990s to teach newly arrived immigrants modern Hebrew in Hebrew.

I was thoroughly imbued with Judaism from the eighth day of my life. I went to religious services religiously–not much choice there–attended Sunday schools and after-school Hebrew classes, partici-pated in all the Jewish communal functions, went with dad to endless weddings, funerals, hospital and home visits to the sick and dying, listened to Jew-ish orators till my ears pounded. But still, I never considered myself particularly religious. God and I had a wonderful relationship: We left each other alone. Be a rabbi? Sure. When the Messiah comes.

I came out of the U.S. Navy in 1946 and had no idea what I wanted to do with my life. I ended up living in the dormitory of Hebrew Union College while getting my undergraduate degree at the University of Cincinnati. I never felt what so many Protestant ministers describe as the "call." God never put a hand on my shoulder and said, "I want you." I still get jealous of clergy who describe their entry into the ministry or rabbinate in those terms. I did enjoy the social activism, the political controversy in which I found myself, the teaching, and once in a while, the intellectual stimulus one or two of my professors would pro-vide me. I hung in and passed enough courses to qualify for ordination, a title some of my teachers were reluctant to confer, since I was, in the words of one of them, "too much a humanist."

Then I got lucky. A new congregation, Temple Sinai, was opening up in Washington, D.C., and I was asked to be its rabbi. It was love at first sight. I was literally trained by some of the finest civil libertarians, judges, social activists, and practical idealists in American Jewry. That ten-year experience shaped and changed my life. I learned the relationship between caring and real politics. I learned the importance of fact and exactitude when speaking publicly. I learned about hypocrisy and deceit in government. By trying to speak moral truth to power, I learned there were values greater than popularity. I learned the perils of too much candor. It seasoned me for the threats that were to come later. The rabbinate, as it turned out, is probably the greatest career for a person who likes people and who wants to make a difference in society.

So what difference have I tried to affect in these five decades? First, to make this place we call society just a little better than it may have been before I got here. Second, to champion reason as the way to find and know anything about Divinity and the place God occupies in the cosmos and in our lives. People should not have to check their brains at the door when they enter a church, syn-agogue, or mosque. If what is being said from the pulpit does not make sense, if it does not square with what we have learned in the lab or by look-ing through a telescope at the heavens, we should not be buying what is said from that pulpit. Belief comes after inquiry, not before or in spite of it.

This is not a good time to advocate reason as a basis for faith and action. We are now into "caring" and "feel good" justifications for religious identity and affiliation. Few who occupy pulpits wish to challenge government or use their pulpits to question political actions. Visible involvement in matters such as a women's right to choose, gun control, the destruction of our environment, the greed of corporations are all issues from which clergy and congregations flee. I wonder if I would drift into the rabbinate nowadays. What so many of my colleagues seem to have settled for doesn't fit my style.

ELIEZER BROOKS

Congregation Boneh Y'rushalayim, New York City

I was born in Colon city, Panama, the descendant of Jewish great-grandparents on both my parents' sides. At the end of World War II, I left Panama as a baker on the U.S. Army hospital ship "The Republic." On board, I regaled the captain and crew with my rendition of "Danny Boy" and other popular songs. Partly because of this rapport, the captain helped me with the legalities of settling in the United States.

I found lodging in New York City, at the corner of 30th Street and 8th Avenue, and attended the nearby West Side Synagogue. I attended the City University of New York and graduated with a degree in psychology. I became a teacher, with a special emphasis on teaching disabled youth. I soon heard about a congregation in Harlem, Rabbi Matthews' Ethiopian Hebrew Congregation. When I went, Rabbi Matthews discovered that I could read the Hebrew prayers, and he asked me to be his cantor. He later asked me to represent him at a benefit concert. Some of the greatest Jewish cantors of the time participated in the concert. I sang the selection "A Dudele," by the composer Leo Low. I was last on the program, and when I was finished, the audience stood and shouted for more.

In 1960, I decided to attend Yeshiva University's Cantorial Institute, and studied there with Dr. Carl Adler, one of the great Jewish musicologists of the time. I was the only student who looked like I did–black-skinned. Some students showed their dislike, but by and large, most people accepted me as I am. I was there to learn, and as long as I was taught the same way as everyone else, nothing else bothered me. I forged very strong relationships there, some of which remain until today.

When I met people at Jewish functions–and especially when I was introduced as "Cantor Eliezer Brooks"–people would often react with a look of astonishment and say something like, "How interesting." After a while, I became afraid to be introduced, but I overcame that feeling. I came to understand that that was the price I had to pay–and I paid it.

I realized that if I was going to help the dark-complexioned Jewish people, I would have to be able to set up my own curriculum of studies. So I organized Congregation Boneh Y'rushalayim in the Bronx. It was incorporated on April 13, 1963. Soon after, D'vorah Lapson from the Jewish Education Committee of New York visited the synagogue and suggested we send a group of our children to participate in a citywide Jewish Dance Festival she was organizing. The children from our synagogue were received well and continued to participate in this annual event. Lapson later invited the children from Boneh Y'rushalayim to march on the first Salute to Israel Parade in New York.

In 1972, I was ordained as a rabbi at the Beyt HaMidrash L'Rabonim in Brooklyn. I have officiated at weddings, birth ceremonies, and funerals. At all times, I have tried to be concerned with the welfare of everyone I have come in contact with. My psychology degree helped me in this regard, making me a better rabbi and better leader for the people of my community, by teaching me to deal with their everyday stresses and concerns.

And so I live as a cantor and as a rabbi. As a cantor, I am the messenger of the congregation in prayer. As a rabbi, I am something of a social worker to my community.

ANGELA WARNICK BUCHDAHL

Assistant Rabbi and Cantor, Westchester Reform Temple, Scarsdale, N.Y.

Rabbi Buchdahl
is the first
Asian-American
woman to be
invested as cantor
or ordained as
rabbi from Hebrew
Union College.

*"I promptly decided,
at sixteen, that I
wanted to be a rabbi.
I saw the life of the
rabbis on the trip,
and I wanted that
life for myself, the
life of learning and
the life of question-
ing and probing."*

I was born in Seoul, South Korea, to a Buddhist Korean mother and a Jewish father who was in Korea for work. I was born there and lived there until I was five. I then moved to Tacoma, Wash., where my father's family lived, and I joined my father's synagogue at age five. My father's family had been affiliated with this synagogue for a hundred years, and I felt like I was part of the establishment when I got there. It was a warm, embracing congregation, and there was never a question that I would be considered fully Jewish—even though Jewish law historically has said that people are Jews only if their mothers are Jewish, or if they undergo conversion.

I went through the religious school program there, and when I was fourteen, I went to Camp Swig in California, which was a Reform movement camp. Our synagogue didn't have a music teacher anymore, so they sent me to this camp and said, "Learn as much as you can, so you can come back and teach music." Music was such a big part of how I connected to the synagogue as a child. I felt it was terrible that we did not have a music teacher anymore. So I learned a lot of Jewish music in camp, and I started teaching when I was fifteen. That was the beginning of my life in Jewish music. And the camp experience itself was also very powerful.

The following summer, I went to Israel on the Bronfman Youth Fellowship, and that changed the direction of my life. The learning I did that summer was challenging, interesting, intense, and spiritually probing. I promptly decided, at sixteen, that I wanted to be a rabbi. I saw the life of the rabbis on the trip, and I wanted that life for myself, the life of learning and the life of questioning and probing.

But it was also, at the same time, a very painful summer for me. The program is multi-denominational, and I had an Orthodox roommate. We discussed how we were going to observe Shabbat in our room. She said she could accept my opinion, but said, "You're not a Jew." I had never converted, and my mother is not Jewish,

and that was the first time I'd encountered people who did not consider me Jewish. But I came out of that summer thinking, I am as Jewish as anybody else, and I am never going to undergo a conversion ceremony.

I had dealt for years with questions of whether I was Korean or American, and that summer, questions of my Jewishness started to factor in as well. I faced serious questions about how Jewish I was, because I met people on the trip whose lives were so wholly Jewish: They listened to Jewish music, and they had Jewish hobbies, like knitting yarmulkes in their free time. That was so foreign to me; in many ways, Jewishness was something I did when I went to a certain place. Many things were infused in me, but it was hard to recognize them.

That trip influenced my decision to go to Yale for college. When I went there, I encountered a lot of Jews like those I had met in Israel. I questioned my whole sense of Jewish authenticity.

Then it became clear to me that Judaism was in me in ways I had not even understood before. Saying I would not be Jewish anymore was as ridiculous as saying I would not be Korean anymore; it was just who I was.

Despite my earlier protestations to the contrary, I decided to have a conversion ceremony when I was twenty-one. I called it a Gior, by which I meant a re-affirmation ceremony. I made peace with the acknowledgment that half my family is Korean and that my mother's influence on me is not Jewish. I wanted to make an active choice to affirm my Jewishness, which I think is a very powerful experience for anybody. It was a very important ritual for me; it transformed me.

To a certain extent, I wear on my face the struggle that many American Jews go through, with their competing identities. For me, it was being Korean, American, and Jewish, but for others the struggle is about being a feminist or homosexual. We live in a complicated world and we are complex people. My Jewish identity journey is at the same time unique to my experience and also one that so many other people have been on.

MICHAEL COHEN
Rabbi Emeritus of the Israel Congregation in Manchester Center, Vt.

Rabbi Cohen lives in Manchester Center, Vermont, where he serves as the Rabbi Emeritus of the Israel Congregation in addition to doing his work for the Arava Institute for Environmental Studies and the Keren Kolot Education Center of Kibbutz Ketura. He is a past President of the Reconstructionist Rabbinical Association.

"Both Judaism and baseball are concerned with the return home. Both recognize that sacrifice is one of the ingredients for that return. And both teach that failure is part of the journey."

On one wall of my synagogue office was a collection of quotes. Tidbits of wisdom and insight; instant lessons or something for someone to read when the phone rang and I needed to answer it. One quote belonged to John Hammond, the great music entrepreneur who discovered Dylan, Springsteen, and others. I also read his quote from time to time from the pulpit: "I am still a New Yorker who owns no house, who thrives on city weekdays and country weekends. I still would change the world if I could, convince a nonbeliever that my way is right, argue a cause, and make friends out of enemies. I am still the reformer, the impatient protester, the sometimes-intolerant champion of tolerance. Best of all, I still expect to hear, if not today, then tomorrow, a voice or a sound I have never heard before, and something to say which has never been said before. And when that happens I will know what to do."

A contemporary film director said that without imagination there is no hope. We all live with imagination and hope; those dreams we carry. They may stop us from falling asleep at night, but also get us out of bed in the morning wondering if the next letter or email or phone call will be the one we have been waiting for. Some are grand dreams; *fantasies* might be a better a word. Some are less grandiose and therefore more obtainable, but still a dream.

It is one of the reasons why saying *brachot*, blessings, is so important. Through blessings we transform the ordinary into the unordinary. The finite touches the Infinite. Through *brachot* we see our lives and our actions in a larger setting. It is therefore not surprising that the rabbis of the Talmud teach us to say a minimum of a hundred blessings daily. But even a *bracha* doesn't work without imagination.

Every year my family and I make the trip from Vermont to Chicago to visit Alison's parents. Chicago is a great city: great restaurants; great museums; and great sights. There is my favorite street, Devon Street with its Indian Restaurants, Jewish bakeries, and Jewish Bookstores. Ah, some chapatti right out of the oven and a new Torah commentary. What more could one want! And then there are sports. Chicago is one of the best, if not the best, sports cities in America.

To paraphrase Leo Durocher, "Baseball is a lot like synagogue. Many attend, few understand." One of our tasks as rabbis is to narrow that gap. Rabbi Jack Cohen says, "If you don't understand baseball, you can't understand life." Both Judaism and baseball are concerned with the return home. Both recognize that sacrifice is one of the ingredients for that return. And both teach that failure is part of the journey. A good baseball player who bats .300 fails 70 percent of the time. As Rav Steinsaltz reminds us, "We should regard the faults or failures as something constructive, like the beginning of a new and beautiful story." And in the annual Torah reading we don't make it into the Promised Land. Rather we get a glimpse across the Jordan River at the end of *Sefer Dvarim*–Deuteronomy–and then roll the Torah and start all over again from the Beginning.

A few years ago, my son Roi and I went to see the Chicago White Sox. Dave Justice was at bat, and he hit a foul ball. Before I could get nervous and think about dropping it, and as it began to arch its way down on its trajectory, I put out both bare hands and caught it. I stared at it, saying to myself in disbelief, "I caught a foul ball!" I then raised my hand with the ball to the crowd who cheered me on. I thought about tipping my yarmulke to the crowd but decided not to. Roi was elated. Father and son moments don't get much better. He held onto the ball the rest of the game, but I did tell him that it was mine. He already has two baseballs from Wrigley Field, but those are other stories.

As the game went on and I continued to drink in the excitement of what had happened, I translated the catch into a metaphor about life. It's about when our dreams come our way. Are we ready to catch them and not drop them? And that is the exciting thing about life; we never know when that ball, that dream, that vision, that hope may come our way.

RACHEL COWAN
Director, Jewish Life Program, The Nathan Cummings Foundation

Rabbi Cowan is the Director of the Jewish Life and Values Program–a department within the Nathan Cummings Foundation in New York City. Through her leadership, the Foundation has invested substantial resources to support Jewish renewal and renaissance in Israel, the former Soviet Union, and the United States. As a convert to Judaism and now a rabbi, Rabbi Cowan is heavily involved in outreach to interfaith couples.

"I came to value he role of teacher, leader, and community builder, and decided to go to rabbinical school. I was forty-three when I entered the Hebrew Union College."

G rowing up in a 1950s New England Protestant family in the Boston suburbs, I was active in the Unitarian church. I found my spiritual connection in nature, but I liked the community of meaning that the church provided. It was not about a belief in God or finding meaning in God. I felt a community of values about politics and social values.

Then I married Paul Cowan, who was Jewish–and very passionate about being Jewish–but was neither religious nor knowledgeable about Judaism. Religion was not something we thought much about until we had two children. We thought the children should know something about Judaism, but Paul did not know much about it. We started a small, once-a-week Jewish school. It was a lovely community of people and very inclusive; they never marginalized me because I was not Jewish. The more I learned, the more I liked what I was learning.

Paul's parents died in a fire in 1976 when our children were fairly young. Their death turned my attention toward larger questions of meaning. I decided to explore Judaism deeper, though I didn't really think of converting because I did not think I believed in God. But I began to be very interested in questions about God, and God's role in the world. After several years, I decided Judaism was the path through which I would explore these questions. Then I understood that conversion was the identification of that path rather than the arrival at the end of it.

And so I converted in 1980 and started to work at a synagogue on Manhattan's Upper West Side. The synagogue, Ansche Chesed, was falling apart, and I helped coordinate a group of young people from the neighborhood who were interested in revitalizing the synagogue. I came to value the role of teacher, leader, and community builder, and decided to go to rabbinical school. I was forty-three when I entered the Hebrew Union College.

My goal was to be a congregational rabbi. But at the beginning of the fourth year of my five-year ordination program, my husband was diagnosed with leukemia; he died a year later. I decided I was not prepared to take on the leadership of a community, as I had a lot of healing to do myself. I started to work at the 92nd Street Y and later was offered a job directing the Jewish Life program at the Nathan Cummings Foundation, a philanthropic organization established by the founder of the Sara Lee Corp.

In rabbinical school, I wrote my thesis on the attitude of Judaism toward healing. I discovered there was a lot of work to be done helping people move through and beyond loss and grief. The Jewish community had handed the role of comforter and advisor to those who are ill over to the rabbi, to make hospital visits. Many rabbis had not been well-trained in this work. One of the first projects I became involved in at the foundation was the creation of the Jewish Healing Center, which continues to provide resources to Jews suffering illness or loss.

In recent years, I have become very interested in reviving the contemplative tradition within Judaism, and I am beginning to develop a serious contemplative practice that focuses on meditation, study, and prayer. The main teachers of meditation have been Buddhist, but in fact it is a tradition that has always existed within Judaism. For me, the contemplative practice has been focused on understanding the still, quiet voice of God in daily life.

Until Paul got sick, my spiritual path was one of joy at learning and celebrating. With Paul's illness and death it matured into a more complex path that explores the shadow side of joy–loss, grief, doubt, and ultimately healing and comfort. I delved into trying to understand God's presence in the dark places, how to understand and accept the death of a young, vital person–and go on without giving up or losing faith. I have come to understand that a full spiritual life encompasses joy and despair, celebration and grief, the fullness of life and death.

We all need to discover the Jewish spiritual resources to help us. We are blessed with wise prayer, a long history of hope overcoming fear, of rituals and holidays, and of community. They provide us the framework to reach out past the fears for our own safety to connect with God and with our higher purpose–fulfilling God's vision of a world informed by truth, lovingkindness, and justice. A world at peace.

ELLIOT DORFF

Professor of Philosophy, University of Judaism, Los Angeles;
Vice-President, Academy of Judaic, Christian, and Islamic Studies

Rabbi Dorff, Ph.D., is Rector and Distinguished Professor of Philosophy at the University of Judaism in Los Angeles. He is Vice-Chair of the Conservative Movement's Committee on Jewish Law and Standards, and he has served on a number of federal government commissions on health care issues. He is the author of nine books including *Matters of Life and Death: A Jewish Approach to Modern Medical Ethics.* He and his wife, Marylynn, have four children and one grandchild.

"With my writing, I strive to apply the Jewish tradition to modern issues so that its viewpoint and values can live in our lives."

Camp Ramah, the Conservative movement's summer sleep-away camp, was undoubtedly the single most important factor in my decision to become seriously Jewish and, ultimately, to become a rabbi. I went for the first time when I was twelve, and for the first time I saw Judaism lived twenty-four hours a day. At that time you had to be taking at least six hours a week of Jewish studies during the year in order to be accepted to camp, and so I continued my Jewish studies after my bar mitzvah the next year. When I was fifteen, Rabbi David Mogilner led a series of weekly discussions on issues in Jewish thought. He was a rabbi who had devoted his life to Judaism, and yet he was on the attack, asking us why anyone in his or her right mind would believe or do any of the things Judaism stood for. That showed me that you did not have to turn off your mind to be seriously Jewish, but that on the contrary, Judaism welcomes probing, questioning, and even skepticism. I later earned a doctorate in philosophy, but even then intellectual honesty and rigor were important to me, coupled with the warmth, wisdom, and joy that I found at Ramah. I ultimately became a rabbi because I wanted to share the spoils, to show others how rich, challenging, warm, and wise Judaism is.

Ever since I was ordained, I have been working with rabbinical students, teaching them, counseling them, and becoming their friend. Clearly one aspect of what I have hoped to achieve, then, is producing rabbis who love Judaism as much as I do and can communicate that feeling in an honest, effective manner. I consider it an inordinate privilege to have taught and come to know hundreds of rabbis since I began directing the rabbinical program at the University of Judaism in 1971.

The other part of my work is my scholarship, including nine books and over 150 articles on Jewish thought, law, and ethics, with a specialization in bioethics. With my writing, I strive to apply the Jewish tradition to modern issues so that its viewpoint and values can live in our lives. I understand my writing as just another form of teaching. Jewish medical ethics demands that everyone aid in the healing of others, and so for the past twenty or thirty years, I have also tried to embody this value by giving blood four or five times a year and, during the last year, by giving blood platelets used in curing cancer patients.

My service on the Conservative Movement's Committee on Jewish Law and Standards, on which I have served since 1985, has led me to write some fifteen rabbinic rulings (*teshuvot*), applying the Jewish tradition to modern issues. Some of those rulings have later become the basis of chapters in my books, and I am indebted to the members of the Committee for their intelligent and helpful suggestions. It has been a joy to participate with them in addressing some of the most important issues concerning living Judaism in the modern age.

Probably the most interesting things I have done as a rabbi center around my service on several federal government commissions: the Ethics Committee of Hillary Rodham Clinton's Health Care Task Force (1993), the Surgeon General's commission to craft a Call to Action for Responsible Sexual Behavior (1999–2001), and now the National Human Resources Protections Advisory Commission of the Department of Health and Human Services to review and revise the federal guidelines dealing with research on human subjects. I have also testified in front of President Clinton's National Bioethics Advisory Commission on the issues of cloning (1997) and stem cell research (1999), shedding light for them on ways in which the Jewish tradition speaks to these issues. While these have certainly been exciting and, I hope, of use in formulating American policy on a number of important issues, I still love most my interaction with students in and out of the classroom.

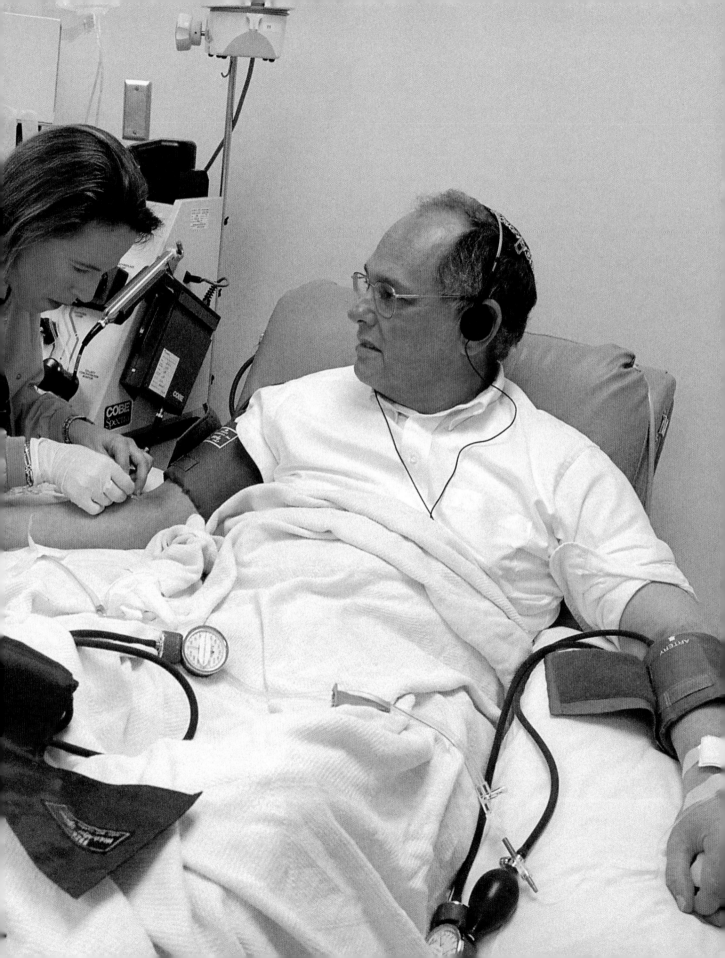

ARIEL EDERY
Congregation ATID, Barcelona, Spain

Rabbi Edery was born in Argentina and moved to Israel at age eighteen to study at Hebrew University. He then lived in Mexico City for five years, working at diverse Jewish institutions. He is married, with twin five-year-olds, Maaian and Eyal.

"To present a liberal and open way of Jewish religious, cultural, and con-gregational life is a challenge, for it is something almost unknown to most Jews here, and certainly some-thing new to the general society ..."

I was born and raised in Buenos Aires, Argentina, and after high school I moved to Jerusalem to study at Hebrew University. My wife and I then moved to Mexico City, where I worked within the Jewish community as an educator for five years. My next move was to Cincinatti, where I enrolled in–and was ordained at–Hebrew Union College. During my time at the seminary, I was contacted by the ATID congregation in Barcelona, Spain, and I made several visits there while still a student. After being ordained, I moved to Barcelona and became the congregation's full-time rabbi in 2001.

The synagogue here is very young, in many ways: It is just five years old, and I am the second full-time rabbi to be here; the typical member is in his or her late thirties or early forties. There are altogether about seventy families and fifty singles, all from very diverse backgrounds. Jews were expelled from Spain in 1492, were only admitted in a very limited way in the twentieth century, and were granted full religious freedom only after 1978. Our congregation, therefore, is formed mostly by first-generation immigrants, mainly from Latin America, but also from France, Israel, the United Kingdom, and America.

An important–and growing–segment of our members are Jews-by-choice, those who converted to Judaism. In Spain, this is a very particular phenomenon (and a moving one from my Jewish perspective) which is the result of Spain's troubled relationship to Judaism. There are many people who know, or find out, that their families are of Jewish origin, but whose true religious identity was hidden or repressed, often for generations and even centuries. Some families retained small shreds of Jewish identity, such as candlelighting on Fridays, disbelief in church authorities, and love of Israel. These remnants of Judaism are sometimes enough to spark for the new generation, living in freedom, questions about where these practices come from and what they mean. Welcoming them, helping them connect to actual Jewish culture and life, is a real challenge and a privilege for us.

Our congregation is also particularly significant, for it is the first and only Progressive synagogue in the country. I am the only non-orthodox rabbi in Spain. To present a liberal and open way of Jewish religious, cultural, and congregational life is a challenge, for it is something almost unknown to most Jews here, and certainly something new to the general society–which in some degree still holds a distorted view of Judaism and Jews, and never had the chance to even meet actual Jews.

I must say that in the brief period of our activity here, we have made serious and big steps, and have begun to fill the gaps. We are actively engaged in interfaith dialogue, in opening our doors to all, and we are reaching the general population by means of cultural activities and celebrations that we promote and arrange. Local media and institutions are particularly receptive now to our activity, and they very often turn to us to hear our voice, or to present our culture in different forums.

It is hard to be a small minority within Spain, and it is hard to be a minority among the Jews, too, since most are secular and not yet involved in Jewish life. However, when I sit to study with Jews who have come back to our people after centuries of oppression, when I see in the synagogue young artists, kids, and adults eager to hear every teaching and tradition, I am confident about the future and proud to be part of this revival of Jewish life in this beautiful country that is once again becoming a home for us.

DENISE EGER

Rabbi, Congregation Kol Ami, West Hollywood, Calif.

Rabbi Eger is the founding rabbi of Congregation Kol Ami, West Hollywood's Reform Synagogue. Rabbi Eger has been at the forefront of creating a welcoming and inclusive place for gay men and lesbians and their families within the Jewish community. She has worked extensively with people with HIV and created programs for children of gay and lesbian parents.

"As a parent, I want my child to grow up in a Jewish community that continues to tie our spirituality to our work for social justice on many fronts— and for him to feel that same sense of connection to God, Torah, and Israel that guided me."

I believe that serving the Jewish people as a rabbi is a privilege. From the youngest age, my parents' own involvement in Jewish life set an example of the importance of being of service to God and to our community. I know their hard work on behalf of the synagogue and other Jewish organizations made an important mark on my own young life.

I was born in Pennsylvania, but raised in Memphis, Tennessee. The Jewish community in the South was highly affiliated and there was a great connection between the community members. There was a sense of piety and dedication to the synagogue. Our rabbis were men of learning, kindness, and they reached out to me. This feeling of belonging is exactly what I strive to instill today in my own community.

As the founding rabbi of Congregation Kol Ami in West Hollywood, California, I find that so many of our congregants are seeking connection and roots, a sense of linkage to history and community. Many congregants were disengaged from Jewish life until they found Kol Ami. Our congregation is a way back into the Jewish people. I hope to create a holy space that can foster these ideals along with a strong commitment to our Jewish heritage.

So many of the Jews I have come into contact with since my ordination at Hebrew Union College in 1988 are looking to our tradition for uplift, comfort, guidance, and hope. In particular, my work with gay and lesbian Jews and people with AIDS has reinforced this need. Our traditions and teachings that remind us to include rather than exclude, to welcome the stranger, to visit the sick, to free those who are captive guide my work with this community in particular.

I have been most proud of my ongoing work through the years to include gay men and lesbians in Jewish life. From the struggle to have openly gay men and women be ordained as rabbis to the issues of marriage and weddings, I have worked to insure that all Jews are welcome in our Reform movement. I have served as chair of the Task Force on Gays and Lesbians in the Rabbinate of the Central Conference of American Rabbis and

as co-chair of the Gay and Lesbian Rabbinic Network. I have written numerous articles on the issues of human sexuality and continue to work in this area.

As a parent, I want my child to grow up in a Jewish community that continues to tie our spirituality to our work for social justice on many fronts—and for him to feel that same sense of connection to God, Torah, and Israel that guided me. I pray that I will be able to serve the Jewish people for many years to come.

HAROLD EINSIDLER

Ritual Director, Park East Synagogue, New York City; Bible and Talmud instructor, Rabbi Arthur Schneier Park East Day School

Rabbi Einsidler is Principle of the Leon and Gina Fromer Park East Religious School. He has served as an instructor in Bible and Talmud at the Park East Day School for thirty-two years. His enthusiastic sounding of the shofar traditionally heralds the High Holidays.

"It is within the grasp of our Torah educators, despite the obstacles we face, to change the complexion of American Jewry to adhere to the tenets of our faith."

According to Jewish tradition, a father is not just a biological entity, but the Torah demands that a father must be the one who transmits to his child the covenant of Abraham–the 613 commandments of the Torah and our Jewish heritage as a whole. The Torah mandates that the fathers should be the prescribed teacher and mentor. If due to circumstance this cannot be done, then a teacher must be procured to act as an agent for the father.

The Torah teachers on the American scene today have an awesome responsibility to transmit the heritage in this sophisticated technological age. It is compounded by the fact that many of our students have little or no Jewish tradition and identity transmitted to them in their homes, so whatever they learn in school is contrary to their family's lifestyle.

Today's Torah instructors cannot just impart knowledge in a positive and enjoyable way, but must also translate that knowledge into Jewish action and experience, whereby the students can be emotionally stimulated and hooked on to live Jewishly. Therefore, Shabbatonim (weekend retreats), holiday-oriented workshops, and youth programs with Jewish themes must be implemented.

It is within the grasp of our Torah educators, despite the obstacles we face, to change the complexion of American Jewry to adhere to the tenets of our faith.

MOSHE EISENBACH
ZACHARY EISENBACH
Scribes

Written by Zachary Eisenbach, in memory of his father.

Rabbi Moshe Eisenbach is considered one of the most prominent scribes in the world.

His son, Rabbi Zachary Eisenbach, runs a shop on Essex Street, in the Lower East Side of New York City, near his father's old Norfolk Street shop.

"My father, may his memory be blessed, was a very holy man. He never cheated anybody. The most important thing I learned from him was that you have to be soft and patient to everybody."

My father was born in Jerusalem, where I was born also. We came here in the late 1930s, when I was only a boy, too young to remember the trip and our life before it. My father was the fourth generation born in Jerusalem, which is rare, since most Jews in what is now Israel immigrated there only during the past hundred years. But he decided to move to the States because of economics. We came here for *parnassa*–you have to make a living.

We settled on the Lower East Side of New York, where so many thousands of immigrant Jews lived. He lived in the neighborhood until he was very old. My father opened his *sofer*–scribe's –shop on Norfolk Street, where he worked until his death nine years ago. A scribe writes the Torah scrolls, mezuzas, teffilin, and so much else. It is difficult work. If you are at all nervous, you can't do the work: You can drop the ink, and ruin what you are making. You have to be *mechabed* for Hashem–honoring God with your work at all times and with every stroke you write.

The shop was always called Eisenbach. We were never ashamed of our name. It was always a small shop. As a child, I used to watch my father work in the shop, observe how he was working. I learned everything about being a sofer from my father. When I got older and became a rabbi and sofer myself, we worked together for a time. It was beautiful, working together, the two of us alone together, with our two hands. Today, my shop is on Essex Street, still in the Lower East Side, just blocks from where my father worked for so many years.

I became a rabbi because I was following my father's footsteps. I studied at Yeshiva Torah Vodaath and Beis Medrash Elyon, two important American Torah-study academies. My father did not care what I did and never pressured or even asked me to follow in his footsteps; he would have been happy with whatever I liked. I did it because I liked it, and I became a sofer like my

father because I love the work. The Lower East Side neighborhood is very different now, but somebody has to continue doing the work here. We still have plenty of Jews here.

All the great rabbis used to come and buy my father's products. Rabbi Moshe Feinstein, one of the greatest rabbis of the twentieth century, regularly bought by my father, and today, his son, Reb Dovid Feinstein, comes to me. Rabbi Kaminetzky, another great rabbi of the previous generation, used to come here as well. All these major rabbis knew my father. He was a very giving man and everyone loved him. He made a big impression on everyone.

My father, may his memory be blessed, was a very holy man. He never cheated anybody. The most important thing I learned from him was that you have to be soft and patient to everybody. Whenever someone needed something from the shop but couldn't afford it, my father would give it to him for nothing. That's how I try to run my business also–straight, no fooling, nothing dishonest.

You don't get rich on this sort of work. It's plain work. Like my father, I do it for a more important reason than money. I work as a professional, but not money-wise. It's holy work, and I enjoy it; it is a mitzvah, and I enjoy doing mitzvot.

Zachary Eisenbach

LT. COL. SHLOMO GARBARCHEIK

Chief Rabbi of Non Combatant Armed Forces in Israel

Rabbi Garbarcheik is a rabbi in the Israel Defense Forces and is part of the army's disaster rescue unit.

"The reason for my interest in this position derives from an inner calling to foster an interest in Judaism and to put people back in touch with their Jewish roots and identity."

I began my army career as a military rabbi twenty-five years ago. The reason for my interest in this position derives from an inner calling to foster an interest in Judaism and to put people back in touch with their Jewish roots and identity.

My work with Israeli army soldiers began even before I enlisted as a military rabbi: On various holidays I visited soldiers in the field, wherever that may have been, to celebrate with them, and also to give lectures on Judaism and lend an open ear for discussions and counseling.

In the framework of my position as a military rabbi, and especially during these last nine years as rabbi of the Home Front Command, I am the resource person for all matters of Jewish concern—a similar role to that played by local community and congregational rabbis throughout Israel. I help arrange dietary law observance, Sabbath observance, study groups, lectures, personal counseling, arbitration in matters of the application of Jewish law to everyday issues, and the establishment of new synagogues. The main part of my work is to listen and provide an ear for any and all matters of concern to soldiers of the Israel Defense Force.

In the course of my various duties, I participated in Operation Litani and in Operation Peace for the Galilee, both in Lebanon. In that capacity, I was called upon to provide answers for many contingencies, including setting up synagogues in the field and other similar matters.

Of special interest is my work for six years as the rabbi for the Gadna (literally: Youth Brigades), intended to provide military training and know-how to high school youth prior to their official induction into the army at age eighteen. At that time, I made special efforts to serve as communications facilitator between religious and secular youth, so that they could get to know each other better. In that capacity, I worked as coordinator for the World Bible Contest (Youth Division), which is held in Israel every Independence Day. I envisioned this contest as a bridge between Jewish youth from Israel and the Diaspora: Study of the Bible brings them in touch with their Jewish roots and their ancestral homeland, and hopefully I was able to assist in this endeavor.

AKIVA GARBER
Scribe

Rabbi Garber is a very popular rabbi known as the "Jerusalem scribe."

"All of Jewish life is—or ought to be—lived in constant engagement with the sacred, but it is nonetheless unusual in our world to have such an immediate and concretely creative relationship to sacred things."

A rabbi is a Jewish teacher. As you learn and live Torah, you become better able to express your true being through Torah and mitzvot and better able to help others see how they, too, can do so. As a rabbi, you counsel and teach others about Torah and what it mandates for someone in their situations. The rabbi helps integrate the eternal Torah into the lives and thought of each specific person in a way appropriate for them, making space for us to express God's will and work in our lives and in our being.

Learning Torah is both an intellectual and a spiritual activity of great depth and scope. As the Mishna states in *Pirkei Avot*, the Ethics of the Fathers: "Turn it over and turn it over, for everything is in it." In studying and teaching Torah, one participates in the exposition and expression of God's teaching in our world. This entails creative engagement and conscientious explication, interwoven with innovative insight. Through participation in the age-old chain of tradition you become a part of it, clarifying and refining it, and interpreting it to yourself and to others. Teaching Torah is a great pleasure, for its own sake as well as because it is a pleasure to assist others in clarifying their thought and increasing their understanding. Relationships developed in mutual study and practice of Torah and mitzvot are often intense and lasting, creating an ever-expanding web of international Jewish community. With the mobility and the technological tools of our time, these relationships are maintained and developed worldwide.

Also in my work in The Jerusalem Scribe, I have continuing contact with Jews and Jewish communities from around the world. (We have even sent mezuzas to Ghana and China!) I regularly answer all sorts of questions addressed to us through our web site, JerusalemScribe.com, and I teach and demonstrate Jewish calligraphy and scribal arts to students and scribes, rabbis and restorers, tots, teens, and adults.

Through my work as a *sofer*, a Jewish scribe, I experience a special relationship to *kedusha*, sanctity. Living in close contact with *kedusha* alters one's consciousness. All of Jewish life is—or ought to be—lived in constant engagement with the sacred, but it is nonetheless unusual in our world to have such an immediate and concretely creative relationship to sacred things. A scribe creates and works with sacred objects, which acquire their sanctity through his investing it in them. By restoring old Torah scrolls after they have become invalid for use, we return them to life. In the process, I am one of the few people who still studies Torah directly from the parchment scrolls. Furthermore, constant involvement with the details of *sofrut*—the art of being a scribe—has brought me intimate knowledge of this branch of Torah, which I teach and share.

GERSHON MENDEL GARELIK
Chief Chabad Rabbi of Italy

Rabbi Garelik is the Chief Rabbi of Italy and the spiritual leader of Merkos L'Inyonei Chinuch-770. He is one of the most influential leaders in the world Chabad-Lubavitch.

"Today, I am often stopped in the streets of Milan and asked questions. When the political situation in Israel is precarious, people often stop me just to say 'We're with you.'"

Being a Lubavitcher Hasid is the most important aspect of my life. My essence is so intertwined with that of the Rebbe that I constantly feel the Rebbe's presence in all I do.

Before I was married, I lived in New York, near the Rebbe, and so I did not make my decision to go overseas as an emissary lightly. My heart's desire for years had been to be as close to the Rebbe as possible, but I nevertheless decided to leave–but promised myself I would return as often as possible.

Before I left, the Rebbe gave me several copies of the Tanya–a central Lubavitch text–and told me to give them away to the congregants I would serve in my new community. He then added a couple extra copies, saying that someone may need them on the airplane. My wife and I looked at each other in wonder: Would someone really need this *on the plane*? But as good Hasidim, we asked no questions.

Sure enough, not long after takeoff, a young man came over to me and asked if I had an extra Tanya to give him. It was an omen of things to come. I noticed that whatever the situation, I felt the Rebbe at my side.

I was once invited to a city in Europe to attend the inauguration of a yeshiva. As a participating rabbi, I prepared a Talmudic speech that I had heard from the Rebbe. But one of the prominent guest rabbis, who was speaking before me, stood up and started a similar talk to the one I had planned. What to do now? All of a sudden the speaker an elderly rabbi, faltered and stopped talking, so when my turn came, I finished the speech to the satisfaction of the previous speaker.

Today, I am often stopped in the streets of Milan and asked questions. When the political situation in Israel is precarious, people often stop me just to say "We're with you." Once, having recently returned from New York, I was walking home from synagogue, meditating on the Rebbe's words that "G-d is to be found down here on earth." Suddenly, a car of young men pulled up; one jumped out–I never found out whether he was Jewish or not–and asked without preamble, "Where is God to be found?"

Taken by surprise and not wanting to enter into any conversation, I just pointed to the sky with my finger. The young man ran back to his car. As I walked on, I reflected on my answer and was upset with myself for not having answered in the way the Rebbe had said. In that moment, the same car came around, and again this young man jumped out and called, "Where is G-d to be found?" This time, I pointed my finger toward the ground, as if to say, "God is found here on earth." The young man lifted his thumb and said, "Just the answer I was looking for."

The first time the Chanukah Menorah was lit in one of the main piazzas of Milan, some people boycotted and voiced a chorus of objections, all along the same lines: "Menorahs are supposed to be lit in the privacy of the home, not in the center of town where people can ridicule it." Today, the local Jewish newspaper describes the first night of Chanukah as "our traditional gathering in Piazza S. Babila." That in a nutshell is what has happened during the past forty years. Jews in Italy are proud to come out into the open and proclaim their Yiddishkeit. As the Rebbe said: "G-d is down here, on the earth."

LAURA GELLER

Senior Rabbi, Temple Emanuel, Beverly Hills, Calif.

Rabbi Geller is the Senior Rabbi of Temple Emanuel in Beverly Hills, California. Prior to this position she served as the Executive Director of the American Jewish Congress, Pacific Southwest Region. Rabbi Geller has received many honors, including Woman of the Year Award from the California State Legislature. She was the third woman in the Reform Movement to become a rabbi.

"In my position now, I feel like I am in a large laboratory, where I get to be part of imagining a synagogue that makes a difference in people's lives."

I was not particularly reflective about my Judaism until I was a student at Brown University in the late 1960s, the time of the antiwar movement and identity politics on campus, when the center of campus political activity was the chaplain's office. These factors encouraged me to think about the role my religious tradition played in my life. I was particularly influenced and moved by two Protestant ministers whose political work came out of their religious commitment. It made me think of the connection between my sense of social justice and my religious background.

After my freshman year, I attended a Southern Christian Leadership Convention gathering in Memphis. It was the year after Martin Luther King Jr. was assassinated, and being at this conference that was primarily African American and predominately Christian was a very powerful experience for me. But I felt like I did not belong there. At that moment I realized I had a community, my Jewish community.

After my sophomore year, I dropped out of school and lived on a kibbutz in Israel. That experience was pivotal for me, in both it helped me understand the extent to which my Judaism and my being an American were central to my identity. That experience compelled me to go back to college and study Judaism seriously, and I ended up at Hebrew Union College's rabbinical school.

I was ordained at HUC as the third woman in the Reform movement to become a rabbi. It was an interesting transition from a university environment, where feminist concerns were part and parcel of everyday life, to a seminary that had not yet confronted the impact of feminism on Jewish tradition. After ordination, I became the Hillel rabbi at USC, where I served for fourteen years. When I turned forty, I noticed I was spending an increasing amount of my time dealing with faculty and administration members, tackling issues of diversity and pluralism on campus, and less time with undergraduates. I realized it was time to move on. I then became the regional director of the American Jewish Congress, where I served for four years. It was a fascinating time

to be a community leader, and we did a lot of groundbreaking work: We held the first Muslim-Jewish dialogue, and created a Jewish feminist center and a Jewish urban affairs center.

Over the years, I married and had children and could not find an adequate synagogue in which to educate my children. I began to realize that if synagogues do not work, we are not going to be able to transmit a meaningful Judaism to the next generation, no matter how important the work of all other Jewish institutions may be.

In 1994, the position of senior rabbi of Temple Emanuel emerged. When I had been a student in seminary, I knew I did not want to be a pulpit rabbi; but, two decades later, I decided to pursue the Temple Emanuel position, and I was selected as the first woman to serve as the senior rabbi of a major metropolitan congregation.

It has been a very exciting time to be the rabbi of a large congregation. The buzz-word of the Jewish community is synagogue transformation; there is a real sense that the foundation of Jewish life in America is the synagogue. In my position now, I feel like I am in a large laboratory, where I get to be part of imagining a synagogue that makes a difference in people's lives. The way this has taken shape at Emanuel is through a different notion of leadership. Many synagogues developed with a hierarchical model, in which the rabbi is at the top of a ladder, with a clear sense of authority. The model evolving at Emanuel is one of shared leadership–between me and the other synagogue professionals, as well as a strong sense of shared leadership between the professionals and the lay people. The goal of the professional leadership is to empower the lay leadership to become more self-sustaining Jews, and to help them be able to lead services, teach, and mentor each other. We want to create a community that is shaped much more like a wheel, not a ladder.

To me, being a rabbi means helping people notice the divinity that is present in their lives, and helping them honor the Torah of their own lives–and understand it in the context of the Torah of our tradition. It means empowering people to take responsibility for their own Jewish lives.

MARC GELLMAN

Senior Rabbi, Temple Beth Torah, Melville, N.Y.; cohost, "The God Squad"

Rabbi Gellman (pictured on left with Monsignor Thomas Hartman) is part of the nationally known television team called the God Squad. He earned a doctorate in philosophy from Northwestern University, and has written several award-winning children's books. With Monsignor Hartman he has co-authored, *Where Does God Live?* and *Religion for Dummies*, among others. Rabbi Gellman is the immediate past President of the NY Board of Rabbis.

"As rabbis, we do not work for any of the 'them's that fill the life of a rabbi; none of these 'them's could bring forth the effort and the commitment that mark the life of a rabbi: the willingness to be present at all times and the courage to speak the unpopular truth."

The most challenging aspect of this calling–for such a sacrificial and sustaining passion cannot conceivably be called a job–is to remember always that you work for God and not for them: Not for your family, not your congregation or Hillel campus group or hospital or prison or nursing home, not for the needs and causes your work funds and fulfills, not for those who need us in Israel.

As rabbis, we do not work for any of the "them"s that fill the life of a rabbi; none of these "them"s could bring forth the effort and the commitment that mark the life of a rabbi: the willingness to be present at all times and the courage to speak the unpopular truth. We rabbis–like priests and ministers and other God workers–work for God and for no one else.

Our work for the Jewish people is only a result of the fact that God has touched and commanded this people. Our work with congregations is only a result of the fact that that those are the spiritually organic institutions we created, after the fall of the Temple in Jerusalem, to worship God. And our work with individuals in joy and grief is only a result of the fact that we are sent to help people see their own burdens and blessings as just the lines that flow from God into and through them.

When I came to the interview with the congregation I have now served for almost a quarter century, I told them what my teacher, Rabbi Jacob Wolf, had said to his congregation at the beginning of his tenure there: "There will not be a single day when I think I work for you. I work for God. And the reason I believe this–and the reason I must believe this–is because if I worked for you, I would have to do what you want. But if I work for God, I can do what you need."

Trying to remember that soaring and transforming truth has been the hardest part of the rabbinate for me. Every day there are temptations to spin the truth into a more digestible gruel, to pander to the rich, to excuse the poor, to accept the needs of congregants for me to be their surrogate Jew and to live their Jewishness through me and not because of me–because of what I have taught them about what God wants each and every one of them to do with the blessings given to them and not to me.

I am sustained by the knowledge that faith is trust, not knowledge, and that the impact of whatever goodness has not been leached out of me by my arrogance and sin would reach out to God through all of them. I know God made me do this. I used to care if I did it well. Now I only care that I do it with love and a good heart. Of all the Jewish texts that come to my mind, none come closer than this passage from Shakespeare to the truth that only goodness endures and sustains a rabbi: "What! A speaker is but a prater; a rhyme is but a ballad. A good leg will fall; a straight back will stoop; a black beard will turn white; a curled pate will grow bald; a fair face will wither; a full eye will wax hollow: but a good heart, Kate, is the sun and the moon; or, rather, the sun and not the moon; for it shines bright and never changes, but keeps his course truly" (*Henry V:* Act V, Scene II).

EVERETT GENDLER
Rabbi Emeritus, Temple Emanuel, Lowell, Mass.

Rabbi Gendler is the Jewish Chaplain and Instructor in Philosophy and Religious Studies, Emeritus, Phillips Academy, Andover, Mass.

"Such "innovations"–more accurately, the reclaiming of the natural vitality originally found in those liturgical celebrations–have touched, excited, delighted, and moved many people to a fuller appreciation of Judaism and a deeper concern for nature."

I t seems quite natural that a descendant of Abraham and Sarah should ask himself the question: What am I doing here? What is my purpose, my task, my mission here on this earth? After all, their original dislocation was a response to their Divine assignment. Appropriate, then, that those of us who follow their path–though obviously at different turns and with different footsteps–should ponder such questions. And the answers–more precisely, the intimations, the intuitions, the insights–are more likely to lead us aright, not astray, in so far as they take account of and reflect our personal circumstances.

I was born in Chariton, a small Iowa farm town (pop. 5,000), and lived there my first eleven years. As I look back at those years, I am struck by three features of life there that I think partially marked my path and defined my task for the following decades: the omnipresence of the Iowa countryside, with its black, fertile soil, gently rolling prairies, miles of corn fields, and expansive skies; the importance of the practice of Judaism within our home, but–with only three Jewish families in Chariton–not primarily as part of a larger Jewish community; and my awareness of being different from other kids because I was Jewish, though I also had a sense of belonging and being rooted in those natural surroundings.

One discernible result is that I have developed over the decades a passion for integrating elements of nature into Jewish religious practices: special attention to New Moons and Full Moons; a sun wheel and special poetry at Sabbath services nearest Solstices and Equinoxes to mark the turning of the seasons; the conversion of our Temple Emanuel Eternal Light to solar power more than twenty years ago. Such "innovations"–more accurately, the reclaiming of the natural vitality originally found in those liturgical celebrations–have touched, excited, delighted, and moved many people to a fuller appreciation of Judaism and a deeper concern for nature. They were helped, I am convinced, by a certain personal marginality, my sense of the validity of Jewish individuality not confined to accepted community practices. And their contribution to the religious lives of many Jews and the preservation of our planet reflects, surely, something of the purpose of my being here.

Two formative experiences during adolescence also, I believe, contributed significantly to some of my life-long religious commitments. When we moved to Des Moines, my involvement with our local synagogue and its rabbi, Monroe J. Levens, introduced me to both the classical Biblical prophets and current social issues. Amos, with his passion for economic justice and his challenging, gutsy rhetoric, was my overall favorite; Zechariah, with his vision of God's Spirit effectively replacing might and violence as the effective agency for achieving social justice, was most intriguing. Acquaintance with some deeply convinced Iowa Quakers and the American Friends Service Committee solidified my tentative commitment to the struggle for social justice by nonviolent means, and this, too, has been a significant part of my sense of religious purpose on this planet.

Throughout adolescence, I had the experience of being moved and inspired by music, by poetry, by paintings and sculpture, by philosophical writings, and by plays. Often the inspiration from an especially affecting piece of music or writing felt similar to what I received from my Jewish religious tradition, a feeling powerfully reinforced during the amazing, eyes-ears-and-spirit-opening years when I was a student at the University of Chicago. Understandable, then, that the Sabbath services I later conducted would include selections from Haim David Thoreau, Reb Meir Rilke, e. e. cummings, William Blake, Carl Sandburg, and others. How should Mozart's 200th *yahrzeit* (anniversary of his death) not be taken note of at our Shabbat service? How should Gandhi's birthday pass unnoticed? *Yi-chud* (a central Jewish value) will mean little if it does not begin with our bringing together in harmony those various elements that contribute to the life of our own spirit. This, too, the recognition of the sacred beyond the confines of any single tradition, its acknowledgment, and its inclusion in our own religious expressions, has been for me a decades-long conviction and practice that I now regard as part of my mission.

JACOB GOLDSTEIN
Chief Chaplain of the New York Army National Guard

Rabbi Goldstein holds the rank of colonel. He currently serves as an Assistant Commissioner of Housing for the State of New York and is Chairman of Community Board No. 9, where he has served for more than twenty years. He is also Chaplain with the U.S. Secret Service and sits on many boards and institutions.

"I spoke a few minutes at each service, and said, 'We're standing before holy ground, because everyone who died was an innocent civilian.' We blew the shofar, and my hands trembled."

On Rosh Hashanah of 2001, I held services at Ground Zero, the site where the World Trade Center had stood just days before. They were open to everyone in the vicinity who wished to participate. In all I held six services–three each day of the Jewish New Year festival.

They were not long services, because of the mission. People were in a rescue mode; they were happy to participate, but they had to go back to what they were doing, digging in the rubble looking for survivors and bodies. I spoke a few minutes at each service and said, "We're standing before holy ground, because everyone who died was an innocent civilian." We blew the shofar, and my hands trembled.

I witnessed the airplane fly into the second tower, and I was stunned looking at the scene. Listening to the radio, I realized we were basically under attack. Within an hour and a half, I received a call that the Army National Guard was being mobilized, and that I needed to prepare to bring my chaplains in. I immediately sprang into action: I called my assistants and my wife grabbed my gear, and I reported to where we were meeting.

As the senior chaplain, my job is mainly administrative–making sure the chaplains are all covered, and that I know about all the issues that arise in their work. The second part of my mission is being down there to help deal with the grief of our soldiers and the others participating in the mission. People's emotions go with the various phases of the work, the various ups and downs: The high is trying to find somebody alive, and of course, now all we're doing is searching.

To help our soldiers cope with the disaster, we tell them that they should look at a brighter tomorrow. Their very presence means they are giving hope and protection to others, that they are an inspiration to others. One oft-asked question is, Why did God let this happen? The answer I give is that God is good, but there are evil people. Here they can see evil at its worst.

The scene at Ground Zero is much different from what I experienced in my tours of duty overseas as a chaplain. I've seen tours of combat in Granada, Desert Storm, and also in Kosovo and Bosnia more recently. There, the deaths we experienced were not all in one place and not from a faceless, gutless enemy that attacks civilians. We faced armies and knew who the enemy was.

In a personal sense, I deal with the tragedies by trying not to think too much about what I am doing. I am able to say Psalms for strength and inspiration, and I know I am doing what my Jewish values demand I do. The first Shabbat after the September 11 attacks, I was digging in the pile at Ground Zero. Someone asked me how I could do that on the Sabbath, when digging is forbidden. I responded by referring to the Talmud, which says that if a wall of stone collapses and people are trapped underneath, you are required to desecrate the Sabbath to try to save them. If you are there, you are obliged to help, and if you do not assist in the rescue effort, it is criminal in the eyes of God.

I've been a chaplain since 1976. A chaplain is the religious and moral conscience of a command. As a chaplain, I bring that part of the world to the soldiers. I started at the lowest rank of chaplain. Today I am the state staff chaplain, the head of the New York National Guard chaplaincy. I am the first Jew in this position, and my job is to mentor and pastor to other chaplains, most of whom are not Jewish. I counsel people from all walks of life, and all kinds of backgrounds.

Being in combat is a very different situation than being a chaplain at other times. Because of the pressures of combat, soldiers are much more eager to talk to you than during peacetime. During Desert Storm, I was assigned to the Patriot missile unit, so I left my usual unit and went to Israel. There, I was the senior task-force chaplain. I remember when the ground war started; we'd gotten a secret briefing when the war was going to start. It was very somber, very quiet. It was two or three in the morning, and a group of soldiers came over to me and said, "Can we pray with you, chaplain?" I couldn't even see who they were. It wasn't important or even relevant to them what I believed in, and it was irrelevant to me what they believed in. From a small group, it grew, simply because that's how soldiers are.

NILES ELLIOTT GOLDSTEIN

Author; chaplain; founder, the New Shul, Greenwich Village, New York City

"I have always tried to harmonize the call of the wild with the call of my faith. But now, as the rabbi of a new synagogue in New York City's Greenwich Village—called the New Shul—I have discovered a deep and profound source of fulfillment that my earlier adventures only hinted at."

I have always viewed spirituality, like life itself, as a great adventure. If, as Kierkegaard argues, God is the Absolute Frontier—or what the Kabbalists (Jewish mystics) call "The Boundless One"—then our quest to experience the Transcendent will always be an unpredictable one. Spirituality, the ongoing and evolving relationship between human beings and God, is often marked by certainty, gratitude, and joy. But it can sometimes be punctuated by doubt, despair, even anger. Still, as long as we are engaged with God, we are living out a spiritual journey as real as that of our biblical ancestors.

For me, religion represents the concretization of the divine-human relationship. The rites, rituals, and ceremonies of Judaism are meant to link one with the other, to serve as kisses between heaven and earth. Although as a progressive Jew I believe that religion is a human construction, I do not believe it was created in a vacuum. Religion is the response of our forbears to the powerful reality of God, their faithful attempt to fathom who God is and what God wants of us.

My rabbinate has been my own attempt to figure out how I am supposed to serve God, and it has been a bit eclectic. I have worked as a chaplain for the federal law enforcement community, counseling agents and cops in squad cars and on bar stools; I have run a "cyber-synagogue" for the Microsoft Network, teaching about Judaism in the ether of the Internet; I have done my own version of missionary work, meeting with Jews in remote and war-ravaged regions like Central Asia and the Caucasus; and I have led young Jewish men and women on challenging Outward Bound-style canoeing and rock-climbing trips in places as disparate as Nevada, New Jersey, and Alaska's Arctic National Wildlife Refuge.

I have always tried to harmonize the call of the wild with the call of my faith. But now, as the rabbi of a new synagogue in New York City's Greenwich Village—called the New Shul—I have discovered a deep and profound source of fulfillment that my earlier adventures only hinted at. For in the end, Judaism is as much about serving each other as about serving God. In fact, since in Jewish theology human beings are viewed, and should be treated, as images of the divine, the two are inseparable. That is what it means to become, as the Torah urges us to be, a kingdom of priests, a holy nation. It is *avodah*—sacred service—that truly defines the observant Jew, the serious and life-transforming commitment and devotion to help other people, to heal our fractured world, and to heed the responsibilities of the covenantal relationship with our Creator and Redeemer.

YOSSI GORODETSKY

Executive Director, European and North African Bureau of Lubavitch, Paris

Rabbi Gorodetsky was born in Brooklyn, N.Y., and received his rabbinical ordination in 1989. From 1986–87, he directed Youth Outreach programs in Great Britain. Since 1992, Rabbi Gorodetsky has been the Executive Director of the European and North African Bureau of Chabad Lubavitch in Paris.

"They were in need, essentially, of assistance in all aspects of starting a new life after the terrible tragedy they lived through."

T he situation in Europe in the post-war years was horrible. There was hardly any food available, and there was practically no housing. In this respect, the situation in Paris was the worst in Europe.

Realizing this, the previous Lubavitcher rebbe, Rabbi Yosef Yitzchok Schneerson, opened in Paris the central office for his activities in Europe and North Africa, and for certain activities and projects in Israel. At the head of the office, he placed my grandfather, Grand Rabbi Benjamin Gorodetsky. The Rebbe appointed him as his personal emissary for Europe, North Africa, and Israel. At the time, he dealt primarily with refugees from Eastern Europe who were coming from the Displaced Persons camps. The first task was securing visas for our brethren living in the DP camps and getting them safely to Paris. They were then placed in lodgings in Paris and the surrounding areas.

It was then obviously necessary to create various institutions for these newcomers, such as schools, and to assist the refugees with gaining employment. They were in need, essentially, of assistance in all aspects of starting a new life after the terrible tragedy they lived through.

My grandfather and the bureau he headed also provided the necessary items needed to observe the Jewish customs and laws, including the Jewish holidays. In 1948, Ireland donated three million pounds of meat as a gift to the Jewish refugees. It was necessary to organize rabbis and *shochtim*–ritual slaughterers–to ready this generous donation for the needy refugees. The bureau trained many shochtim specifically for this occasion, and many are still active in their trade today.

The bureau also created a school to train *sofrim*–scribes. Today, many of these scribes are working in Israel and Europe. At the time, the American Jewish Joint Distribution Committee (JDC) retrieved from Germany 1,200 Torah scrolls that had belonged to the ravaged Jewish communities of Eastern Europe. These scribes, trained by our school, were given the task of checking, verifying, and repairing these holy

scrolls. Many communities in Europe and Israel benefited from their work.

At this time, other schools also were created, such as the Yeshiva for Higher Education and Rabbinical Studies in Brunoy, France, and the Beth Rivkah Girls School and Teachers Seminary in Yerres, France. Today, Rabbi Gurevitch–who was sent to France by the previous Rebbe–is the director, along with Rabbi Schonthal, of the Beth Rivkah school, which remains the only Jewish girls' school in France to provide dormitory facilities.

The village of Nachlat Har Chabad in Israel was founded by Grand Rabbi Gorodetsky upon the request of the then-Rebbe, Rabbi M. M. Schneerson. The desire to expand the presence of Jews in our holy land, as well as the need for housing at the time, made it an important proposition for the Israeli government, which assisted in the development of the town. The well-known town of Kfar Chabad in Israel was strengthened by the many people sent from Paris by the Lubavitch bureau there, and the town continues to thrive today.

In addition, the Rebbe was greatly concerned at the time about the Jews of North Africa, and as a result, Grand Rabbi Gorodetsky founded many institutions there. Whole communities were transformed; in Morocco and Tunisia, for instance, thousands of students were enrolled in the schools he established.

In 1992, I was sent by the Rebbe, with my wife and daughter, to Paris, to assist my grandfather with his responsibilities. At the time, my grandfather was no longer able to travel because of his health, and he needed assistance with the heavy workload his role demanded.

Today there are more than 700,000 Jews living in France, and Chabad-Lubavitch has community outreach centers, schools, and synagogues in every major city. These centers serve all the needs of the local Jewish communities, as well as the surrounding areas that lack an organized Jewish community. Chabad now has more than sixty institutions throughout France, Morocco, and Tunisia, with more than 7,000 children in its schools.

LYNN GOTTLIEB

Congregation Nahalat Shalom, Albuquerque, N.M.

Among the first ten female rabbis ordained, Rabbi Gottlieb is a renowned story-teller, author, and peace advocate. She is a leader in the Jewish Renewal movement, a new Jewish group focused on blending tradition, social activism, and spirituality, such as meditation and chanting.

"Sensitivity to minority rights was the cornerstone of the Judaism of my youth and has continued to shape my practice and view of Jewish life and culture."

I owe the initial unfolding of my rabbinic path to Rabbi Steven Schaefer, who inspired youth of his Reform congregation in Allentown, Pennsylvania, to respond to the difficult and painful reality of the destruction of European Jewry and the struggle to end the practice of segregation in America.

Sensitivity to minority rights was the cornerstone of the Judaism of my youth and has continued to shape my practice and view of Jewish life and culture. I was also blessed with a mother who became a puppeteer and started a children's theater school. From an early age, I drew upon my passion for poetry and theater—and the art of collaboration that theater entails—in the creation of Jewish liturgies that opened the door to the discovery of my own voice.

During a service on Shavuot—the Festival of Weeks—in 1965, Rabbi Schaefer called me to the podium after I delivered a sermon entitled "Man and the Moral Law." The sermon caused the congregation to clap its hands in approval, and when I approached the bima, Rabbi Schaefer whispered the words that changed my life. Someday, he told me, I would become a rabbi.

The death of my beloved mother in 1971 further deepened my sensitivity to suffering and the importance of caring community. In the summer of 1973, I began my journey as a pulpit rabbi at the request of Temple Beth Or of the Deaf in New York City.

The deaf community taught me the beauty of sign language as a perfect instrument of prayer. During those years, I encountered for the first time the *havurah* movement (which encourages small-group, informal prayer), Jewish feminism, the gay and lesbian movement, Jewish mysticism, the interfaith peace community, nonviolence as a religious practice, earth-based spirituality, alternative Jewish education, and the Jewish theater community.

As one of the first seven practicing women rabbis, I was thrust into a national arena that required thoughtful responses. I realized that so many Jewish people of my generation were alienated from a tradition and people that I love. I continued experimenting through creative liturgies, storytelling, and peace work to find ways of engendering a Jewish community open to the voices of all those who felt they had no voice.

In the spring of 1983, a group of unaffiliated Jews asked me to move to Albuquerque, New Mexico. I decided to take a risk and help shape the congregation of my dreams. Eighteen years later, I am enjoying the fruits of my labor. I am especially proud of the number of artists who have found a home in our community and who bring their skills and talents to the shaping of Jewish culture within the congregation. We dance the Romanian Hora and other traditional Jewish dances to the music of our own Klezmer band that plays at all our events. We produce a Jewish Theater Festival, a Sephardic Festival, and Jewish art shows every year. Our liturgies and holy days are filled with puppet shows, creation pageants, music, poetry, and the voices of the people woven into the fabric of the tradition.

I am also lucky to belong to a community that values open discussion and dialogue, along with a communal process based on the principles of mediation. One of the greatest challenges of a rabbi continues to be the way in which the conflict between Israel and Palestine divides mainstream Jewish leadership from the voices that question the wisdom of certain aspects of Israeli policy. I believe that safeguarding the human rights of Palestinians as well as Jewish Israelis has become one of the most serious ethical dilemmas facing the Jewish nation. I hope that the Torah of compassion and peace will allow us to build bridges of understanding for the sake of the next generation.

IRVING GREENBERG

Theologian; founder, CLAL–the National Jewish Center for Learning and Leadership and the Jewish Life Network

Rabbi Irving (Yitz) Greenberg is President of the Jewish Life Network, a Judy and Michael Steinhardt Foundation. Rabbi Greenberg served as Chairman of the United States Holocaust Memorial Council from 2000–2002. He has written extensively on the theory and practice of pluralism and on the theology of Jewish-Christian relations. His books include *The Jewish Way* and *Living in the Image of God: Jewish Teachings to Perfect the World.*

"The halo of the rabbi's image and role had put me on a plane where they would open up their deepest heartfelt feelings and secrets to a total stranger and accept guidance and involvement from a person who otherwise would have been dismissed as a journeyman psychologist."

W hen I was a neophyte rabbi, fresh out of rabbinical school, with little training and hardly any life experience, I became a part-time, weekend rabbi at the Young Israel of Brookline in the Boston suburbs. I had not yet been elected by the membership and the appointment had not even been publicized. Within a day of the appointment, I received a call to visit a family that had just suffered a devastating loss– the unexpected death of the head of the family. When I arrived, none of them said the obvious: that they were older and far more experienced in life than me. They opened up the most personal and intimate elements of their life, and they asked for my advice.

The halo of the rabbi's image and role had put me on a plane where they would open up their deepest heartfelt feelings and secrets to a total stranger and accept guidance and involvement from a person who otherwise would have been dismissed as a journeyman psychologist. That is a distinctive power of the rabbinate, which has moved me again and again throughout my career. It gives the privilege to share people's deepest sorrows, greatest joys, most personal issues, not as a stranger but as someone to whom they are open to sharing, to receive consolation and wisdom. This aspect is personally the most gratifying element in serving as a rabbi, despite the fact that in my own career, my focus has been in the community-building and communal leadership role of the rabbinate, more than in the pastoral, counselor role.

Initially, I did not plan to be a professional rabbi. In fact, since my wife Blu did not want to marry someone who would serve in the pulpit, I promised her that I would not be a rabbi. (Blu insists to this day that I married her under false pretenses, although she has supported me all along as I changed my personal and professional path.) In my family, you were expected to learn advanced Talmud on a daily basis. One studied Torah purely for its ethics and values. I never attended a professional rabbinical seminary. Rather, I went to a European immigrant yeshiva in Brooklyn for studies in Talmud, and I was able to get ordained there. I planned to be an American historian, and my Talmud study was "Torah for its own sake."

I attended graduate school at Harvard, where I found that my "Jewish interests" were stronger than I had imagined. To satisfy these feelings, I became the weekend rabbi at the Young Israel of Brookline–and loved it. Still, I completed my Ph.D., after which I began teaching history at Yeshiva University. As my (unfulfilled) Jewish interests and feelings deepened, I was attracted to the rabbinate. I was determined to do more Jewishly, but YU resisted my teaching Holocaust and other Jewish studies, preferring that I stick to teaching American and general history. When the Riverdale Jewish Center congregation opened up, I became a full-time professional rabbi.

I believe the primary task of a rabbi is taking responsibility for leading the community. There is also the very special personal and pastoral role in the rabbinate, which I loved. However, I had to give up the pastoral side of the profession when I shifted career tracks again and went into dealing with community-wide problems full-time.

The great challenges of being Jewish today are two-fold: how to live in the open society, with its acceptance of Jews and, as a result, rising assimilation; and how to live in the aftermath of the Holocaust and the rebirth of Israel, which have shaped and redrawn our religious experience. A rabbi should build community and institutions that can sustain Jewish life in a free society. A rabbi should teach Torah and equip Jews to learn, know, and experience high level Jewish living–so they will choose to be Jewish. A rabbi must also teach Jewish unity, Jewish power, and Jewish ethics in light of the Holocaust and of reborn Israel.

My principal other rabbinical work centers on theology. The theological writings have been closely related to the communal and other rabbinic work I have done. Generally, the thrust of my philosophy is the attempt to combine the whole tradition of Judaism with pluralism and affirmation of post-modern life.

ZVI GREENWALD

Educator and Lecturer, Bnei Brak, Israel

Rabbi Greenwald teaches and befriends the many Russian immigrants in the Holy Land.

"What is my secret? Joy. Without simcha—joy—it is impossible to succeed."

I was born in Jerusalem in 1931. I grew up studying in Chabad Lubavitch yeshivas and began teaching when I was only seventeen years old. At first, I taught first grade, but later I taught the higher grades as well.

I lived in Kfar Chabad—the Israeli village populated by Chabad Hasidim. In 1955, a tragedy occurred in Kfar Chabad. Terrorists entered a vocational school and opened fire with automatic weapons, killing three young students and two teachers. Afterward, some people thought the school should be closed permanently, but the Lubavitcher Rebbe said that the opposite should happen. He called for the school to be strengthened in memory of those who were lost. I became part of the expanded staff, and I continue to teach there.

There are hundreds of stories I can tell about angry young boys at high risk for crime and drug abuse who were sent to the school by social workers and who made a complete turn-around for the better in their lives. To this day, I receive dozens of phone calls before each holiday from former students thanking me for saving their lives.

I have eleven children of my own, thank God. I also have many grandchildren; there is a custom of not counting one's grandchildren, so suffice it to say some of my children have even more children than I do.

What is my secret? Joy. Without *simcha*—joy—it is impossible to succeed. That is my goal in life: To bring Jews closer to the Torah and God's commandments through happiness and a joyous heart.

ISSACHAER GUTMAN

Scribe in Meah Shearim, Israel

A doctor from Park Avenue in New York once came to me and requested that I personally write the parchment document that goes inside a pair of tefillin, the leather boxes and straps worn by Jewish men during the morning prayers. This pair was to be for his second son; he had previously bought a pair of tefillin from me for his elder son. This man was of the opinion that I had personally written that first pair, but I did not think so, because for a long time I was not personally involved in writing them.

Still, he faxed me a copy of the tefillin passages from his first son's pair, and I realized that I had, indeed, written them for him. I wondered, though, why he was so adamant that I personally do this for him. Why should it matter? So he explained his reason for insisting on my personal involvement in writing this particular pair of tefillin.

His first son had been irreligious: He did not keep kosher (the dietary laws) and went to an irreligious school. But ever since he started donning tefillin, he has eaten only kosher food, even at school. So the father insisted I personally write the tefillin for the second son, hoping it would have the same influence on him that it did on his younger brother. I have no idea whether I really had anything to do with the elder son's transformation, but I was happy to oblige for the younger son, and I hope, like the father, that it has the same effect.

As a scribe, I specialize in writing not only tefillin, but also mezuzas–the boxes affixed to doorposts–and in examining and repairing Torah scrolls. My son works with me and is most proficient. I was his teacher. There are many scribes with whom I work who learned this craft from me.

Here is a bit about how the process of creating these religious items works: A "proofreader" checks what is written on the parchments. He has to be sharp. Not every proofreader has the ability to write holy texts. I am both a scribe–a writer of sacred texts–and a proofreader. Most of the time I work as a proofreader. If you really do it every day for four or five hours, then you develop the ability to catch mistakes. I have been working as a scribe and proofreader for seventeen years.

My grandfather came from Hungary to Jerusalem in 1914 or 1916, during or before World War I. My father was born and grew up in Batei Hungarin, the Hungarian section of Meah Shearim, the ultra-Orthodox section of Jerusalem. I grew up in a different neighborhood–Geulah–and attended the Etz Haim Yeshivah in Mahaneh Yehudah. My father knew almost everybody in Jerusalem. The religious items store that I have in Meah Shearim used to be my late father's tailor shop.

The family of my father's mother stretches back seven generations in the mystical city of Safed in northern Israel. My mother came from Germany before World War II, in 1933. Her family came from Furth (from Bavaria, the southern part of Germany). They came penniless, but nevertheless able to save their lives, which is obviously most important. I have four children: three in Israel and one in New York. I went to the United States when I was younger with the intention of staying one year, but I ended up in America for seventeen years, where I began my work as a scribe. But now I am back in Israel.

When I returned from New York in 1985, there were around five hundred scribes and only ten proofreaders in all of Israel. Today there are thousands of scribes and more than two hundred proofreaders. People have started to learn about this profession and to take it up. I am so thankful that there is such a need for so many professionals to provide tefillin, mezuzas, and all the other religious items to our people in Israel.

YISRAEL HABER

Director, Beit Chabad-Meor Menachem, Chispin, Ramat HaGolan, Israel; former United States Air Force chaplain

Rabbi Haber was the Chief Rabbi of Alaska from 1973–1976. He was a supervisor for the Israel Ministry of Education from 1978–1987. Today he is Director of Beit Chabad in the Golan Heights, Israel.

"However, the greatest accomplishment of ours while in Alaska was the building of the state's first mikveh (ritual bath)–on an Air Force base, no less."

H aving been born in May of 1948–the same month and year that the modern State of Israel was born–perhaps it is not surprising that my path would have the United States and Israel intertwined. My parents proudly displayed those two country's flags from our windows, as America's Memorial Day and Israel's Independence Day took place at roughly the same time.

Educated in yeshivot and universities in New York City as a third-generation resident of Brooklyn, I was interested from an early age in becoming a rabbi, as a result of the deep respect and admiration I felt toward my uncle, Meir Moshe Haber, of blessed memory. He was the most charismatic individual I have ever met, and I hoped to follow in his path.

Upon marrying my dear wife, Miriam, I soon entered the United States Air Force as a Jewish chaplain. Being stationed in Alaska, I became responsible for ministering to both the civilian and military Jewish communities of the forty-ninth state. I, in fact, was the chief rabbi of Alaska–by virtue of the fact that I was the *only* rabbi in the state.

During the five years I was in the Air Force, I was privileged to travel and meet many Jews in need of a rabbi and to hold services in many exotic locales. I was asked to officiate at a *bris milah* (ritual circumcision) in Bethel, Alaska, 500 miles west of Anchorage; travel to meet Jewish men and women serving on the Azores (islands belonging to Portugal in the mid-Atlantic); help Jews throughout Alaska keep kosher homes and provide them with kosher food products; conduct High Holy Day services in Torrejon, Spain, for Jewish U.S. servicemen and Israeli embassy personnel living in Madrid. So many interesting things happened to us every day that I was asked to publish a book relating my stories; it was entitled, *A Rabbi's Northern Adventures: From the Heights of Alaska to the Golan Heights.*

However, the greatest accomplishment of ours while in Alaska was the building of the state's first mikveh (ritual bath)–on an Air Force base,

no less. The mikveh was built by order of the Pentagon and was realized due to the direct assistance of the Lubavitcher Rebbe, Menachem M. Schneerson. As a result, my wife and I were granted a private audience with the Rebbe himself, a rare privilege. The meeting lasted half an hour. He blessed us and talked to us to raise our morale, and he instructed us to implement many wonderful projects for the Jews of Alaska. That was the first of what would be many visits to the Rebbe. Being imbued with his enthusiasm and holy ways, we knew immediately that we wanted to become close to home. As a result, my wife, our four sons, and I are emissaries of the Rebbe in Israel's Golan Heights today.

We have been living in Israel for the past twenty-four years. We established a "Beit Chabad" (Chabad-Lubavitch center) in the town of Chispin, two kilometers from the Syrian border. I take great pride in meeting with soldiers from the Israel Defense Force stationed throughout the Golan Heights. Visiting with them, especially during holiday seasons, infuses me with a deep sense of purpose.

In 1992, when Israel publicly considered returning the Golan Heights to Syria and the region consequently found itself in the midst of a political cloud storm, I wrote to the Rebbe to convey my concern for the morale and welfare of those living in the region. Within hours, I received the following answer from the Rebbe: "The Lubavitcher Rebbe calls upon all residents of the Golan Heights to be strong–not to be afraid of the recent developments–and to stay in their places with resolve, to build all of the land of Israel, fulfilling their task until the time of the upcoming redemption. Amen."

It is with these words and by that message that my work in the Golan proceeds. I have been privileged to take up the challenge.

YOSEF HADANA

Chief Rabbi, Ethiopian Jews

The descendant
of a long line
of *kesses*–the
Ethiopian Jewish
equivalent of
rabbis–Rabbi
Hadana emigrated
to Israel and
became the first
Ethiopian to be
ordained as a rabbi.

*"My family back-
ground, the know-
ledge I came with,
and the rabbinical
ordination I
acquired in Israel
all contribute to
making me a well-
rounded spiritual
leader to the
Israeli-Ethiopian
community."*

M y father is a *kes*, an indigenous Ethiopian rabbi not officially recognized by the Orthodox Israeli Rabbinate. There have been keses in my family for about eleven generations. But I am the first Ethiopian ever to be ordained in Israel as an Orthodox rabbi.

I was born and raised in the village of Ambovar, Ethiopia, which is near the city of Gondar. This large village was completely Jewish. No one ever violated the laws of Sabbath observance, and our village had the first Jewish school in the whole country. In the folklore of my ancestors, Ambovar was called "the second Jerusalem" because of the intense Jewish life in the village. Today all of the Ambovar villagers have made aliyah to Israel, including my parents and ten siblings.

In Ethiopia, my father was extremely devoted to his work and traveled extensively to villages far and wide–wherever there were Jews. He counseled, taught, and promoted Jewish life. Sometimes he traveled on foot, due to the lack of bus transportation. As a boy, I remember my father leaving the house for Achefer, a place so far away that he was gone for an entire year. His presence in Achefer literally saved the Jewish community, which was on the verge of converting to Christianity. We hardly heard from him, due to the lack of phones, mail service, and e-mail. But as devout people, my family had full confidence that everything would turn out all right.

When I got older, I was sent to Torino, Italy, by the leaders of the Ethiopian Jewish community for rabbinical studies. The Torino Jewish community received me with open arms and gave me a scholarship for my studies. They considered it a privilege and an honor to train Ethiopian rabbis for work back home. I finished my preliminary studies in 1972, when I was twenty years old. Because of the military coup in Ethiopia that year, I was advised not to return home, which I had planned to do. So I made aliyah to Israel that year and continued my rabbinical studies under the sponsorship of Rabbi Ovadiah Yosef, one of the greatest rabbis of our time.

At the end of 1979, I became the first ordained Ethiopian rabbi in Israel. My rabbinical studies enabled me to be of great assistance in solving the religious problems encountered by the new Ethiopian immigrants at that time. Since then I have been serving as the official Chief Rabbi of the Israeli Ethiopian community, responsible for dealing with all of their religious matters–marriage, divorce, preparation for conversion, and a lot of counseling.

My father, who continues to be a most respected leader in the community, is of the utmost help in my work. With his calm demeanor and openness to all, he knows everybody and everybody knows him. Together we provide spiritual guidance for our people. The community recognizes him as the Chief Kes in Israel.

My family background, the knowledge I came with, and the rabbinical ordination I acquired in Israel all contribute to making me a well-rounded spiritual leader to the Israeli Ethiopian community. I accept people as they are and work diligently to solve their problems and concerns. Many couples come to me to solve legal difficulties of Jewish law that prevent them from marrying. After solving these technicalities and officiating at their weddings, I often bump into them several years later–happily married and with children. How happy I am when they remind me of the assistance I was able to give them and when they ask my blessing for their children. This gives me the strength to continue in my work. It is not easy to untangle the knots of bureaucracy, but most times I am successful.

When I immigrated to Israel, I came alone, and there were only a few Ethiopians here then. I personally traveled to the United States and Europe to promote the aliyah of Ethiopian Jewry. There is not a place that I did not go to. Today most Ethiopian Jews are here, and I often have two or three weddings at which to officiate in one night. This makes me happy to no end. How great it is to see our children learning and getting a great education. I have five children of my own–two sons and three daughters. Both sons study in a yeshivah. How much my life has changed from those days in Ambovar; I have so much to be thankful for. It is overwhelming sometimes.

MORDECHAI HALBERSTAM

Spiritual Leader, Congregation Mazah, Brooklyn, N.Y.

Rabbi Halberstam is the rabbi of Mazah, a congregation in the Williamsburg section of Brooklyn, N.Y. He has seven children and one grandchild.

"Being a rabbi means I can help a lot of people. That's my only goal. I don't need anything more than that."

T he Halberstam family is a very well-known rabbinical family and has been so for generations. About 140 years ago, a rabbi lived in Poland by the name of Chaim Halberstam. He was the biggest rabbi of his time, and I am a direct descendent of his. All the men in the generations between him and me were rabbis as well: my father, grandfather, and all the way back.

My ancestor, Rabbi Chaim Halberstam was the Grand Rabbi of Santz, the town in Poland in which he lived. People came to him from all over Europe to ask for his blessings. When he died, his son became the grand rabbi, and it was passed from generation to generation until World War II displaced the Jews from Europe.

My father came to the United States in 1946. He was in his mid-teens when the war started, and he fled to Russia, to Siberia, and then to Paris. Finally, he landed here in the United States and restarted his movement here. He also is the founder of the Jewish Genealogical Institute; he does computer work to discover the roots of Jewish families.

I am his second son, the third of fifteen children. I am among the older ones, and I obviously have much younger siblings as well. I was born in 1958, went to yeshiva for many years, and was ordained at a rabbinical college in Lakewood, New Jersey. I lived in Jerusalem a couple of years, got married, and have lived in Brooklyn ever since.

I am now the rabbi of Mazah, a congregation in the Williamsburg section of Brooklyn. The vast majority of Jews in this area belong to the Satmar sect of Hasidim, and I learned in a Satmar yeshiva until I was twelve. After the Satmar Grane Rebbe, Joel Teitelbaum, died more than twenty years ago, I published a book about him with clippings on his life.

My wife and I have seven children–the oldest is twenty-two, and the youngest is five. Two of my children are married, and I have a grandchild, too. My father is still alive, thank G-d, and has a congregation in Boro Park, another heavily Orthodox section of Brooklyn.

My goal in life is to help people. I help make peace between husbands and wives who are fighting, and I work to settle business disputes as well. In my basement, I have established a center for children who were born with brain injuries.

I recently raised money to renovate the home of a woman who is confined to a wheelchair. I am especially proud of the kitchen she now has. She is able to have some measure of independence. To cite just one example, she can now peer into the pots on the stove via an angled mirror above them; being in a wheelchair, she otherwise cannot see into the pots.

I am also involved in building a new yeshiva in Brooklyn. My children's school needs a new building, so I am helping to raise money and deal with the contractors and other workers. I myself work in real estate, and so I am familiar with that world and am able to help.

Being a rabbi means I can help a lot of people. That's my only goal. I don't need anything more than that. I work with people for the mitzvah of it. I spend my whole day helping people, and it gives me great joy.

I do not own a television, I do not listen to radio, and I do not read English newspapers. I am a soldier of God. I study Talmud a couple of hours a day, and give away most of my days to helping people.

DAVID HARTMAN
Founder, Shalom Hartman Institute, Jerusalem

Rabbi Hartman
is the author of
*Israelis and the
Jewish Tradition:
An Ancient People
Debating Its Future;
A Living Covenant:
The Innovative
Spirit in Tradi-
tional Judaism,*
and other works.

*"After living in Israel,
I rediscovered the
age-old experience
of Jewish history:
uncertainty, loneli-
ness, isolation,
and the concern
for survival."*

F or many years I served as a rabbi in Jewish communities in the United States and Canada. God's power in history was alive to me on Passover, Shavuot, and Sukkot, the three historical festivals. On Rosh Hashanah and Yom Kippur, the imagery of the moral judge of history calling each and every human being to judgment evoked feelings of accountability and renewed commitment. History was not problematic; however meaningful and compelling its dramatic message, it was, in the end, a symbolic history. My theological problems were essentially outside the dramatic events of history.

Providing spiritual understanding for Jews in the modern world is not an easy task. Whereas in the past we shared a common framework of religious authority, today the daily lives of most Jews are not organized by principles of *Halakah* (Jewish Law). What does a believer share with a so-called non-believer?…

Then, suddenly, I was confronted with the frightening events preceding the Six-Day War. The community of Jews in Israel was not the protagonist in a dramatic account of symbolic history but rather a real community of Jews facing the possibility of another Holocaust. And I was impotent to intervene. The reality of a living community in the very midst of the stormy currents of history suddenly invaded my consciousness. I, like most of Diaspora Jewry, was paralyzed with anxiety and dread. Questions of theology and theodicy were beside the point; continuing to participate in the drama of Jewish history seemed unimaginable in the event of another Holocaust. How long could we be witnesses to the silent God of history?

Then, in the aftermath of the victory of the Six-Day War, I felt compelled to come to Israel to find a way of appropriating the reality of the Jewish State. After returning from Israel, when I entered my synagogue on the Ninth of Av, a fast day commemorating the destruction of Jerusalem and the exile, I was struck by the incongruity of my congregants' sitting downcast on the floor reading and mourning for Jerusalem. In the Jerusalem from which I had just returned, Jews were rejoicing in the streets with dance and song.

The contrast was astounding and spiritually maddening. Before the service began, I announced to the "mourners for Jerusalem": "The Jews in Jerusalem are presently jubilant." I was uncertain about whether this meant that identifying with Jewish defeat and suffering, and mourning for the past, had now become meaningless. All I knew then was that my task was to tell my congregation of a reality that could not be easily contained within the confines of the story of Jewish suffering.

Fearing that Jews would lose the powerful significance of the experience of the Six-Day War, I went enthusiastically to my Rav (teacher), Rabbi Joseph B. Soloveitchik, with this request: "Proclaim a religious festival; proclaim God's revelatory presence in history! Must God be revealed only in stories? Can we not celebrate the living God of our directly felt redemption?" Rabbi Soloveitchik responded by referring to a Talmudic passage that says that the festival of Hanukkah, which celebrates the Maccabean victory and the miracle of lights, was not proclaimed immediately after these wondrous events, but rather only in the following year (B.T. *Shabbat* 21b). Pointing out the significance of "the following year," Rabbi Soloveitchik counseled me to wait and not to react in the heat of excitement. His sobriety and restraint were out of tune with the enthusiasm and passion I felt as a result of the experience of liberation.…

Shortly afterward, in December 1977, I left my pulpit and, with my family, went to settle in Israel. After living in Israel, I rediscovered the age-old experience of Jewish history: uncertainty, loneliness, isolation, and the concern for survival. I felt like writing to Rabbi Soloveitchik and saying, "Perhaps you were right. We must wait for 'the following year' before giving an enthusiastic religious response to events in history."

During my rabbinic training at Yeshivah U., I was taught to answer halakhic questions. Upon entering the rabbinate, I was anxious to answer the great halakhic questions of the Jewish community. I waited with anticipation, but to my dismay there were no questioners. Finally I realized that the role of the rabbi was not so much to provide answers as to create questions.

Excerpted with permission from A Heart of Many Rooms *(Jewish Lights, 1999).*

AARON HAUSMAN

Maker of Tzizit (fringes for prayer shawls), Meah Shearim, Israel

Rabbi Hausman is a second-generation tzizit maker. His store is in Meah Shearim, the ultra-Orthodox neighborhood of Israel. He also repairs tefillin and makes tallitot (Jewish prayer shawls). He has five children.

"My mother tongue is Yiddish. I do speak a little Hebrew, but my children also speak Yiddish. We love the old mama lashon *(original mother tongue)—which is Yiddish."*

My father had this store before me, and then afterwards I took it over. I am a second-generation *tzizit* maker. Tzizit are the fringes that are attached to *tallitot*, Jewish prayer shawls, and to the smaller garments worn under the shirt. I've been doing it for over twenty years, and I spent about forty years studying.

Tzizit are so important because, according to Jewish law, all 613 commandments of the Torah are symbolically equivalent to the tzizit (fringes) of the prayer shawl. You see the tzizit and are reminded of all the commandments. My father was also a tzizit maker. He engaged in fulfilling the commandment of tzizit, and likewise I do. Though tzizit do not necessarily need to be made by hand, hand-tied tzizit are more magnanimous.

The store is in Meah Shearim, the ultra-Orthodox neighborhood of Jerusalem. Everybody around here knows me. I sell a few books here and there, a few tallitot now and then, and generally make do. I sit in the store knotting tzizit two hours in the late morning,11:00 a.m. to 1:00 p.m. I rest for an hour after lunch, get up and read a little, and then come back to the store at 5:00 p.m., and work again until 7 p.m. There's not much work to do since there are so few customers.

I was born in the Old City of Jerusalem, where we have been for five generations. All told, we were two brothers and three sisters. My family came from Hungary 140 years ago. My grandfather was born in Hebron. It was my father who came to the Old City of Jerusalem. I studied in Batei Hungarin–the Hungarian section of Meah Shearim. I started out in a *cheder*–a one-room school, often the living room of the teacher–and continued in a yeshivah (Orthodox seminary) and a Kolel (yeshivah for married students).

Though I studied in Batei Hungari, I do not know a word of Hungarian. We've been in the land of Israel for five generations, and Hungarian was forgotten along the way. My mother tongue is Yiddish. I do speak a little Hebrew, but my children also speak Yiddish. We love the old *mama lashon* (original mother tongue)–which is Yiddish.

There is no special reason that I love the work I do, knotting tzizit. My father was here before me and I am continuing his work. I have five children. Only God knows the answer to the question of whether any of them will also be tzizit makers. Now I am in the store myself, an old man of seventy who loves to work and hates to sit idle. That's what keeps me going. I don't have the energy or time to straighten up the store; I'm an old man of seventy years with only a little work energy left. But I know what's in each and every one of the packages here.

ISAK HAZAN

Director, Chabad of Rome

Rabbi Hazan is the Director of Chabad of Rome and the Rav of the Ashkenazi community. He was born in the U.S.S.R., studied in the U.S., and has been in Rome for the past twenty-five years.

"But as Lubavitch, we approached them slowly, and slowly they opened their houses and their hearts, and we became part of the community, and the community began to change."

I n my family, men have traditionally become rabbis. My grandfather and great-grandfather were rabbis, as was my father. On my mother's side, as well, the tradition existed: Her father was the chief rabbi of Odessa, Ukraine, and my mother's brothers were rabbis also. So it runs in the family.

I was born in Moscow. My family originally was religious and observant, but not part of the Lubavitch Hasidic movement, of which I am a part now. We became affiliated with the Lubavitch movement because the only way to maintain religious education in Soviet Russia was through the Lubavitch. They were the only ones who kept up an education system underground, when religious education was illegal. Most other groups gave up. If someone wanted to raise their children in a religious way, they had to look to the Lubavitch. We attended an underground yeshivah in the afternoons, after the regular school day ended.

We immigrated in 1966 to Israel. I was fourteen at the time. Three years later, I went to Lubavitch school in New York, and I did my yeshiva study there for many years. The Rebbe sent me in 1977 to Rome, because many Russian Jews had started immigrating there, and I spoke Russian. It so happened that there was a community in Rome needing a rabbi, so I went there to work with the community–to build up some yiddishkeit in Rome–and to help the immigrants.

There has been a traditional Jewish community in Rome for thousands of years. But unfortunately, they were persecuted for a long time. There wasn't too much education; there was tradition, but not education. After World War II, the people were depressed and scared to identify themselves as Jews. But after we came, we lit the Chanukah menorah in Piazza de Barberini. It was amazing. A lot of people in the local Jewish community didn't want us to do it. In Rome, people were afraid to show too explicitly that they were Jewish; even observant people wouldn't walk in public with a yarmulke.

When we started to light the menorah publicly in this famous piazza in Rome, it heralded a big change. More than a thousand people stood in the piazza, and all the men wore yarmulkes on their heads. People's attitudes started to change. Sunday schools, summer camps, and adult-education programs were organized. It had started before the menorah lighting, of course, but it really picked up steam after that.

There was no real danger in displaying Jewishness publicly, but people were taken aback at first. But as Lubavitch, we approached them slowly, and slowly they opened their houses and their hearts, and we became part of the community, and the community began to change.

In Rome, we have helped Jews from around the world. We have tourists, American medical students, and many others who look to us while they are in Italy. There was one American student who used to come to eat with us often on Shabbos. When he graduated, I did not see him for eighteen years. But he is now a doctor in Pittsburgh, and he came to my son's wedding, which was held in Pittsburgh, and I got to see him again.

In 1979, when the Shah of Iran fell, the Lubavitch had connections in the State Department and were able to get many children out of Iran. The children came through Rome, and I remember the first group. They came alone, to my tiny one-bedroom apartment, and then other organizations came to help them with their papers and other needs. They then went on to the States to study. We got thousands out that way.

We had a lot of Russian Jews who would stop in Rome for a few months before heading to the States, Australia, or Canada. In 1990, I made seders for 10,000 Jews. I couldn't run them myself, so I had help from yeshivah boys from New York. We had financial support from various organizations, but just organizing such a thing was extremely challenging. Each site may have had 800 or 1,000 people. I will never forget that.

AMMIEL HIRSCH & RICHARD HIRSCH

Written by Ammiel Hirsch, shown with his father, seated on left

Rabbi Ammiel Hirsch is the Executive Director of ARZA/WORLD UNION, an affiliate of the Reform movement aimed at spreading Reform Judaism in Israel and around the world.

A champion of civil and human rights, Rabbi Richard Hirsch was the founding director of the Reform Movement's Religious Action Center. As the head of the World Union of Progressive Judaism in 1973, he moved the headquarters of the World Reform movement to Jerusalem and was instrumental in introducing Progressive Judaism in the former Soviet Union.

"One of my greatest pleasures as a rabbi is one I never antici-pated: working closely with my father."

I really had no intention of becoming a rabbi. I went to law school and practiced as an attorney for two years. But at my wedding, I gave a toast, and I spoke about what marriage meant to me. One of my father's friends, who happened to be the dean of a New York rabbinical school, congratulated me and said, "You should really think of becoming a rabbi." And that evening–my wedding night–I told my wife, "I think I am going to be a rabbi."

Until then, I hadn't given it any consideration, but obviously, growing up as a rabbi's son, there was a lot of sentiment in my conscious and sub-conscious awareness that led me to change careers. I felt that there was more I could contribute to society and to the Jewish people as a rabbi than as an attorney. To me, there was nothing more impor-tant than the development and survival of the Jewish people. So I was ordained at Hebrew Union College and worked for three years as an assistant rabbi at Temple Shaaray Tefila in New York.

My family made aliyah when I was fourteen. I finished high school in Jerusalem and then spent three years in the army as a tank commander. I am a citizen of both countries. I am fluent in the cul-ture and society of both countries, in the languages and histories of both countries. So when ARZA–an organization dedicated to developing Reform Judaism in Israel–was looking for a new director, they offered me the position; it was a natural fit.

At ARZA (now ARZA/WORLD UNION), I feel that I am able to put my ideals into practice. Our goal is to mobilize, inspire, and educate members of 900 Reform congregations in North America on Zionism and Israel. We attempt also to rally our communities to build a Jewish future around the world. For example, since the fall of the Soviet Union, we have developed a signifi-cant presence and revitalized Jewish life in the former Soviet Union.

I once organized a group of eighty rabbis to come with me to Jordan and Israel. It was six months before the peace accords were signed between those two countries. We hoped by our presence to show support for the peace process, but the trip was controversial even in our own community, because at the time Jordan was still officially at war with Israel. People asked, What is a Zionist organization doing visiting a country that is anti-Zionist and is at war with Israel? But the Prime Minister of Israel at the time, Yitzhak Rabin, urged us to go, so we ultimately went.

It was a fascinating trip. To get to Jordan, we had to go from Eilat, the Israeli city at the south-ernmost tip of the country, to Nueba, a village in the Sinai Peninsula about two hours' drive south of Eilat. We then took a rinky-dink ferry over to Akaba, Jordan. The trip from Eilat to Akaba should take ten minutes, if you are able to go straight from one to the other. It took us many hours. And after the peace accord was signed, the trip did indeed take travelers only ten minutes.

While we were there, news of our presence seeped out, and we received death threats. There was significant security around us, helicopters were buzzing in the sky, and it was nerve-racking. With all this tension, I hardly slept; I was leader of the group and I was quite concerned the entire time. But on the way back to Israel, we went to Mt. Nebo, where Moses glimpsed the Promised Land in the moments before he died. Just like Moses did, we went up and looked over the Land of Israel. We felt that Jewish history was coming full circle. It was a very moving moment, one of the most memorable of my life.

One of my greatest pleasures as a rabbi is one I never anticipated: working closely with my father. He was the director of the World Union for Progressive Judaism. When we merged the U.S. offices of ARZA and the World Union, my father and I became colleagues for the last year or so before he retired. I had the opportunity to gain wisdom from the fifty years of experience that he had. That was irreplaceable for me.

RICHARD HIRSH

Executive Director, Reconstructionist Rabbinical Association, Wyncote, Pa.

Rabbi Hirsh is the Executive Director of the Reconstructionist Rabbinical Association, editor of *The Reconstructionist*, and member of the faculty of the Reconstructionist Rabbinical College, where he received his rabbinic ordination in 1981. He has served as rabbi of Reconstructionist congregations in Toronto, New Jersey, New York, and Chicago, and was formerly the Executive Director of the Philadelphia Board of Rabbis and Jewish Chaplaincy Service.

"But I soon discovered that if I had a 'calling' as a rabbi— something about which I still wonder— it was not to work with congregants in a synagogue, but to work with other rabbis."

I was nineteen when I decided I wanted to be a rabbi. Back then, I wanted to "teach Judaism," a rather abstract conception: Teach it to whom? In rabbinical school, I managed to get hooked up with a "student congregation," that unique kind of synagogue that is too small or too poor (or both) to attract and hire a "real rabbi" and consequently settles for a rabbinical student. And so when I was ordained, I thought the thing one should do as a rabbi was to teach Judaism to Jews in a synagogue setting.

But I soon discovered that if I had a "calling" as a rabbi–something about which I still wonder–it was not to work with congregants in a synagogue, but to work with other rabbis. For five years I was the director of the Philadelphia Board of Rabbis, an umbrella group comprising rabbis from all of the four major denominations. For the past four years I have been directing the professional work of the Reconstructionist Rabbinical Association (RRA), and teaching future colleagues as a member of the faculty at the Reconstructionist Rabbinical College.

Being a "rabbi to rabbis" is a unique opportunity. I firmly believe that no one but another rabbi–not even the most devoted spouse, partner, sibling, or friend–can really understand the stress and strain, as well as the opportunities to bring holiness into the world, that rabbis experience. The rabbinate today is a profession in transition, serving a community in transition, during a time of transition. Colleagues need tangible and intangible support, everything from advice on contracts and negotiations to resources for managing synagogue politics to materials that can provide spiritual sustenance.

What continues to amaze me is the remarkable diversity of talent, insight, wisdom, compassion, intelligence and ability that can be found among rabbis. Given the differing Jewish denominations, as well as the range of opinions within each one, I sometimes think that all we really share is this title, "rabbi." We diverge, dissent, and disagree about both substantive and silly issues. But transcending our differences is a mutual respect for a covenant of service into which we have entered: service to the Jewish people, service through the instrument of Torah, and service in the name of God.

The typewriter in this photograph belonged to my teacher and mentor, Rabbi Ira Eisenstein. His founding of the Reconstructionist Rabbinical College in 1968 gave me a place to become a rabbi on the only terms I could have imagined accepting: full commitment to the legacy of Judaism, and equally full commitment to open inquiry and the right and need to question what had been passed down.

Rabbi Eisenstein once said of the rabbinate: "It's a demanding job, and sometimes you'll wonder why you chose it–but look at it this way: You get to save the Jewish people." Not a bad way to spend your life.

RICHARD JACOBS

Senior Rabbi, Westchester Reform Temple, Scarsdale, N.Y.

Rabbi Jacobs has been the Senior Rabbi of Westchester Reform Temple since 1991. From 1982 until 1991 he served as the Rabbi of the Brooklyn Heights Synagogue. Currently he is working on his Ph.D. in Ritual Dance at New York University. His books include *The Body of Prayer* and *Forsaking the Status Quo in Scarsdale*. Rabbi Jacobs serves on the Boards of ARZA/World Union, Religion in American Life and Synagogue 2000, where he is also a program fellow.

"Like lifelong Jewish learning and spiritual growth, transformation is never finished but rather always in process."

W hen I was ordained almost twenty years ago at Hebrew Union College-Jewish Institute of Religion, I didn't want to be a congregational rabbi. The Judaism I had encountered while growing up in a large suburban Reform synagogue seemed shallow and uninspiring. The dreary services lacked passion and relevance. Our religious education was woefully inadequate. So how, in good conscience, could I take a leadership role in an institution in which I had so little faith?

But as fate would have it, I am today the rabbi of a large suburban Reform congregation. No, I have not sold out. I have come to believe that it is possible and necessary to transform our synagogues. But change does not come easy.

When I first became the spiritual leader of Westchester Reform Temple in Scarsdale, N.Y., I thought naively that if I could just articulate a compelling vision of what our congregation could become, the members would dutifully roll up their sleeves and off we'd go. With the best of intentions, we made modest changes in our religious school and in our worship, but at best we were just tweaking the status quo. As a former modern dancer who spent years exploring prayer through movement, I have come to view Judaism as an astonishingly beautiful and compelling work in progress. It is an art form, and we are its artists. With discipline and passion we enlist our hearts, minds, and bodies to seek the Nameless One through lives of holiness.

In the last eight years our synagogue has been busy doing the backbreaking work of synagogue transformation. Transforming a synagogue is somewhat like having new owners renovate a home while the previous inhabitants are still inside.

We are still busy renovating our congregation, including the foundation.

Our religious community is built upon five pillars: Talmud Torah, lifelong and life-enhancing Jewish learning; Avodah, personal and communal religious practice, including worship, that fills our lives with spiritual depth; Chavurah, a welcoming, inclusive, and sacred community that embraces each of us with support, care and wisdom; Tikkun Olam, ongoing involvement in bringing healing and justice to the brokenness in our world; and

Klal Yisrael, strengthening our bonds to Israel and the Jewish people in all lands and building commonality among the various streams of Judaism.

Are we finished transforming WRT? Certainly not, but we have learned so much from the work we've done so far. The Experiment in Congregational Education and Synagogue 2000 projects have taught us how to re-envision what we do and given us tools to get there step by step. Like lifelong Jewish learning and spiritual growth, transformation is never finished but rather always in process.

Our congregational journey feels like Joshua and Caleb's brief scouting trip to the Promised Land as recounted in the Bible. When they returned to the Israelites camped in the wilderness, they made their report and showed the whole community some of the fruits acquired on their trip: "We came to the land you sent us to; it does indeed flow with milk and honey, and this is its fruit. However, the people who inhabit the country are powerful, and cities are fortified and very large" (Numbers 13: 27-28). Even with the serious obstacles, Caleb and Joshua were ready to journey toward the land flowing with milk and honey. At WRT, the modest fruits of our efforts propel us to echo Caleb's rallying cry: "*Aloh na'aleh* –Of course we'll get there" (Numbers 13:30).

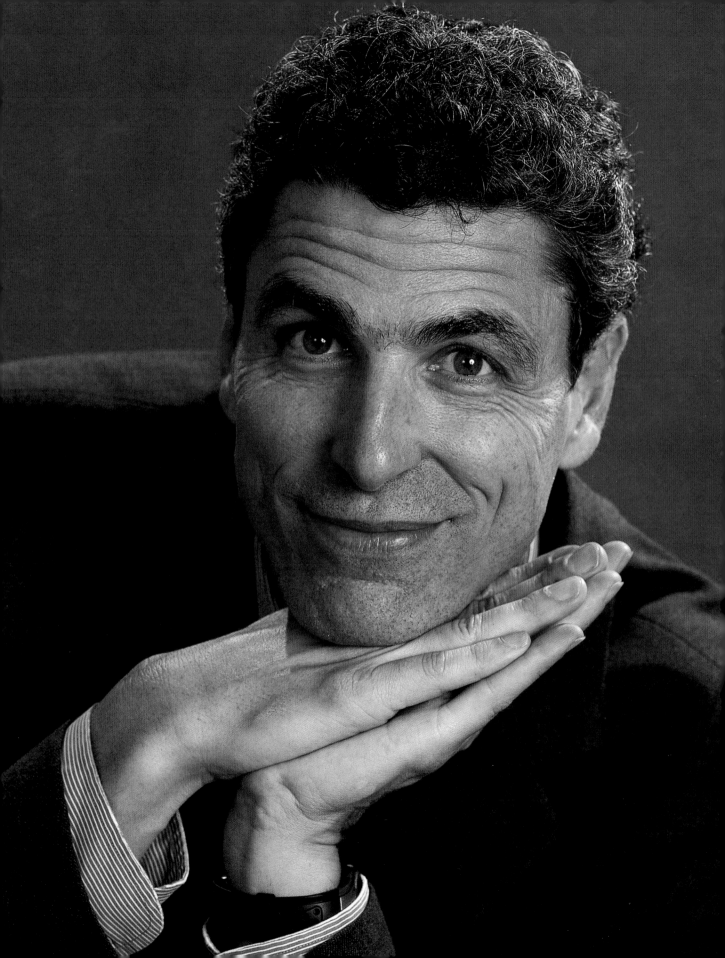

YOSEF KANEFSKY
Rabbi, B'nai David-Judea Congregation, Los Angeles

Rabbi Kanefsky
is Rabbi of B'nai
David-Judea
Congregation in
Los Angeles. He
is also an executive
officer of the
Southern California
Board of Rabbis.

*"There's an old joke
whose punch line
is, 'You're a rabbi?
What kind of job is
that for a nice
Jewish boy?' The
truth is that it is
a wonderful job
and calling, and it
presents opportunities
every day to be a
source of comfort
and blessing..."*

There's no doubt that the rabbinate as a profession presents a trove of challenging situations and demands. But what I have found to be most challenging is dealing with the rabbinate's impact upon my personal life.

There is a unique occupational hazard that attends the rabbinate, and it has to do with personal friendships. Every day I experience the bond of deep, mutual caring that exists between a rabbi and his or her congregants. What is much harder to come by—certainly in the early years in a pulpit—is plain, old, garden-variety friendship. And this difficulty results from one simple fact: I am The Rabbi.

As anyone in this profession quickly learns, rabbi is not something you do; rabbi is something you are. There is no place, there is no time, there is no circumstance when you're not The Rabbi. As a result, every word, every gesture, every joke, is The Rabbi's word, gesture, or joke. Somewhere inside a mere mortal lies, but it would be most unfortunate if character flaws popped out at an inopportune moment. As a result, even in social circumstances, a rabbi needs to especially mindful of everything he says or does. It's hard to make friends when you're always stuck inside The Rabbi.

On a Saturday night during the first year of my rabbinate here, my wife and I went bowling with a group of people from the synagogue. We had a lovely time, but the night did not lack for a tricky moment or two. The most interesting came when one of the members of the group finally managed to get his bowling shoes laced up and began to enter all of our names on the computerized scoring machine, projected overhead. The person was breezing along until it came time to enter my name. His fingers froze at the keyboard.

"Rabbi, how would you like to be entered?" he asked.

Amid the din of bowling balls crashing into pins and video games chirping and buzzing, I faced the question that embodies the personal/professional entanglement. Do I have a first name? Or am I simply The Rabbi?

I tried desperately to think of whether I had ever had a friend who didn't quite have a first name. Nope. There was nothing there. Friends definitely have first names. If this is a gathering of friends, then first names are appropriate. But then I tried to remember if I had ever heard my parents call their rabbi by his first name. No, that too came back negative. And so I smiled self-consciously, and left to his own devices, our scorekeeper—my friend—just entered "Rabbi."

Beyond the general question of personal/professional identity, other specific issues render the rabbi-congregant relationship socially tricky. I am often consulted to render Jewish legal (*halachic*) decisions about the most intimate and personal aspects of congregants' lives. This is a role that all rabbis assume with humility and awe; it is a role he or she is honored to fulfill. But it is not a role that always coexists easily with conventional friendship. On a more day-to-day level, folks want to teach their children to have proper respect for rabbis. And there is nothing like teaching through example. But you want your friends to slap you on the back, not to stand up when you enter the room.

Over the years, I've made a lot of progress. This has been the result of a very conscious effort at deconstructing the invisible social barriers. It becomes obvious very early on that without this kind of effort, a rabbi's life can be a very lonely one—a life filled with caring people but lacking many true friendships. On the other hand, a rabbi's life that includes real friends can be supremely fulfilling.

There's an old joke whose punch line is, "You're a rabbi? What kind of job is that for a nice Jewish boy?" The truth is that it is a wonderful job and calling, and it presents opportunities every day to be a source of comfort and blessing and inspiration to others. You just have to make sure that you get enough hugs as well.

ALVIN KASS

Senior Chaplain, New York City Police Department

Rabbi Kass is Senior Chaplain of the New York City Police Department and Spiritual Leader of the East Midwood Jewish Center, Brooklyn, N.Y. He is a popular author and lecturer and past president of the New York Board of Rabbis.

"As a police department chaplain, I am on call seven days a week, twenty-four hours a day. I work with members of the service of every race, religion, color, and creed; I counsel them at times of stress, both personal and professional."

I n my thirty-five years of service as a chaplain for the New York City Police Department, the September 11 attack on the World Trade Center dwarfed all else I had ever experienced. A couple of hours after the attack, I surveyed Ground Zero to see if I could be of help. The sight was sickening. It was a veritable war zone. The smoke was so thick, I thought it was the middle of the night.

It was incredible to think that those Twin Towers were no longer standing. I recalled an incident from more than twenty years before, when I was called in by the police to persuade a Jewish man not to jump from one of the towers. Fortunately, that episode worked out well.

On September 11, though, I headed from Ground Zero to nearby Stuyvesant High School, where exhausted police officers and fire fighters took time out for a brief respite. The pain and anguish of the ordeal were evident in my conversations with them. They were worried about their colleagues and couldn't understand how anyone could do such a terrible thing.

I proceeded to St. Vincent's Hospital and to Bellevue to visit the injured. I could not believe how quickly both of these great hospitals had mobilized to meet the emergency. At St. Vincent's, a young police officer cried uncontrollably, because what he had seen exceeded anything his imagination could ever have conjured up. I tried to calm parents about the fate of their children who had been working at the World Trade Center.

I was then called to police headquarters, where I stayed until close to 3 a.m. working with my colleagues in the police chaplaincy to offer strength and comfort to families of police officers who were unaccounted for. On the Friday after the disaster, I participated in an interfaith service at police headquarters, during which I was asked to deliver the sermon. In it, I emphasized the strength that all of us acquired from being with each other. The sense of familial togetherness, as well as our faith in God, were the main ingredients that helped us through the ordeal.

As a police department chaplain, I am on call seven days a week, twenty-four hours a day.

I work with members of the service of every race, religion, color, and creed; I counsel them at times of stress, both personal and professional. I am also on the faculty of the Police Academy, where I teach ethics and the sociology of the Jewish community of New York City.

I am also the founding and senior member of the Police Department Ethics Board, which provides insight and guidance to police officers. I help police officers in cases where my status as a rabbi could be helpful. I once persuaded a Jewish hostage taker to give up his guns and release his hostage, who was an estranged girlfriend. The deal-clincher was two pastrami sandwiches from the Carnegie deli in return for each of his guns.

My job is not always solemn. I have had the pleasure of joining together in holy matrimony a multitude of police officers with their loved ones. I am invited to many circumcisions, baby-namings, and bar or bat mitzvahs. I have given the prayer at countless promotion ceremonies–days that are always a high point in an officer's life.

Soon after the September 11 attack, Mayor Rudy Giuliani asked me to participate in a prayer service at Yankee Stadium to remember the victims of the disaster. The event, which was televised all over the world, was unique. To hear supplications in so many different languages and from so many different religious traditions gave me the feeling that the totality of human civilization had come together to respond to these horrific events.

The attack on the World Trade Center brought out the best and the worst in the human spirit. Those who executed this terrible scheme represent the most nefarious ingredient in the human personality. On the other hand, the heroism, courage, self-sacrifice, nobility, and generosity evoked by the attack validate our most profound beliefs in humanity's redemptive potential. These two sides of our character are what Judaism refers to as the *yetzer ha'tov*–good inclination–and the *yetzer ha'ra*, evil inclination. Every person oscillates between these two poles. Our challenge as Jews and human beings is to engage in conduct that promotes the positive side of our nature.

SHARON KLEINBAUM

Rabbi, Congregation Beth Simchat Torah, New York City

Rabbi Kleinbaum is the spiritual leader of congregation Beth Simchat Torah, New York City's synagogue serving the GLBT communities, families, and friends. She lives in Brooklyn with her partner and two daughters.

"…being the openly lesbian leader of an openly gay religious community reinforces my individual efforts to address the political and religious challenges facing our community."

I believe in cosmic influences: I believe that we influence the cosmos, that we influence the world. I believe that what you do, what I do, what we do, matters; our lives, our actions, our words, even our thoughts can make a difference. I believe that we are all here—every one of us–for the sake of what we can do together. Together, we can change the world.

When Jacob Gubbay and a handful of friends started a synagogue in a room in a church annex in Chelsea in the winter of 1973, what they had in mind was a place where they could be both Jewish and gay together. Every fall now–twenty-nine years later–thousands of lesbian, gay, bisexual, and transgender Jews, our families, and our friends from all over our greater metropolitan area gather together at New York's Jacob Javits Convention Center to observe Yom Kippur at services sponsored by that synagogue, Congregation Beth Simchat Torah.

In the ten years that I have been CBST's rabbi, I have officiated at the funerals of leaders of both the New York and the national gay movements, who, following in the footsteps of the Jewish union organizers of a century before, believed they had an obligation to change the world–and they did. I have married couples who understood that such a ceremony was not only an expression of love but also a political act of defiance against a society that still does not accept relationships between same-sex couples as equally valid to those of heterosexuals. I have given blessings over newborns and newly adopted infants of same-sex couples who believe that raising a family is a part of their Jewish heritage that is legitimately theirs, even if the racial and gender makeup of their family does not reflect the community around them. These parents are changing the world; their children and their children's children will change it even more.

I did not become a rabbi in order to be a salesman for Judaism. I became a rabbi because I believe in the meaning and power of prayer and the presence of God in our lives. I did not become a rabbi in order to be a politician or a social worker. I became a rabbi because I believe in the power of religious community to overcome the culture of despair, devoid of meaning and values, in which we find ourselves.

I certainly did not become a rabbi as the result of a positive childhood experience of my religion. After eight years of religious school, I emerged from my childhood ignorant of my faith, illiterate in the texts of my tradition, and distant from my God. The synagogue in which I was raised was, unfortunately, typical of most synagogues then and, alas, even now. It represented what I can only call "pediatric" religion–everything is geared for children. Families join only because membership is required to have their children participate in the bar or bat mitzvah process. Parents bring their children to synagogue, drop them off, and leave. The messages of pediatric religion are all too clear: that religion has nothing meaningful to do with the adult world, that religion does not inform decision making or provide either comfort or inspiration, that religion is an obligation and only done for the sake of the children, and that once you are no longer a child, your only connection to the Jewish community will be to do the same thing to your child.

Like all my openly lesbian and gay colleagues, I am constantly called upon to give advice and support to my heterosexual colleagues both in other synagogues and in Christian churches, as they grow in their determination to acknowledge, celebrate, and honor the life-cycle events of their homosexual congregants. As one of a growing number of lesbian and gay rabbis who are finding our voices and the forums in which we can be heard, being the openly lesbian leader of an openly gay religious community reinforces my individual efforts to address the political and religious challenges facing our community. Lesbian and gay synagogues such as CBST are a constant reminder to the world at large that being gay is not a passing fad, that being openly homosexual and connected to traditional religious practice is not a contradiction in terms, and that a religious community can be something altogether different from what either the secular society at large or the religious right would lead one to believe.

MOSHE KOLODNY

Head Archivist, Agudath Israel Orthodox Jewish Archives, New York City

Rabbi Kolodny serves as the archivist of the Orthodox Jewish Archives, located at Agudath Israel of America's national headquarters in lower Manhattan. An alumnus of Yeshiva Rabbi Chaim Berlin, he has taught Jewish subjects including Talmud at the secondary level and resides with his wife and children in Brooklyn, N.Y.

"The archives I am privileged to maintain are an effective medium for showing different groups of Jews—schools, researchers, authors, and the members of the general community—the contributions of the Judaic heritage."

T hough there are a number of roles played by rabbis, the term "Rabbi" means a teacher of the Torah, a link in the unbroken and continuing chain of Jewish religious tradition and scholarship that dates back to the revelation of G-d to our people at Mt. Sinai over 3000 years ago. The Torah that He revealed to us then is the foundation of all ethical and moral behavior in the world.

In its meaning of "teacher," there is no inherited aristocracy in the title "Rabbi." Anyone who wants to achieve knowledge of Torah and is willing to invest the time and effort to study can become a Jewish teacher. The title is just a credential of qualification. A rabbi can help foster unity among diverse groups of Jews, through the medium of Torah study and observance, as well as through the knowledge and insights he shares with others.

I am not a pulpit rabbi, yet I function as a rabbi by overseeing the Orthodox Jewish Archives, a repository of the history and culture of the priceless Jewish heritage. And so my role is an educational one. The material the Archives acquisitions, arranges, and makes accessible to others is a source of connection between the Jewish past, present, and future, and it bears eloquent witness to how diverse groups of Jews from many lands and cultures are linked to one another through their common beliefs and practices.

Making Jewish historical material available to students and scholars alike is an extremely valuable service. The archives I am privileged to maintain are an effective medium for showing different groups of Jews—schools, researchers, authors, and the members of the general community—the contributions of the Judaic heritage.

And on a personal note, my work as a rabbi not only provides me with direct access to much fascinating and often inspirational material, but it also affords me the opportunity to meet many knowledgeable and interesting people. As they gain from what the Archives has to offer them, I also gain by having my own understanding and knowledge enhanced. And that makes me a better rabbi—and teacher—as a result.

JILL KREITMAN
Director of Education, Central Synagogue, New York City

BENJAMIN KREITMAN
Executive Vice President Emeritus of the United Synagogue of Conservative Judaism; Rabbi, World Council of Conservative Synagogues

Rabbi Jill Kreitman is Director of Education at Central Synagogue, in New York City, and a Professor of Judaica and Rabbi, the University Community at C.W. Post campus at L.I. University.

Rabbi Benjamin Z. Kreitman is a prominent Conservative rabbi. He is an Executive of MERCAZ USA, and Executive Vice President Emeritus of the United Synagogue of conservative Judaism.

"Even at moments of great stress, my daughters would join with me in the study of the Mishnah. Its words would give us strength to overcome the difficulties we encountered."

H appily, it is no longer unique in the Jewish community to see a father and daughter both in the rabbinate. But still, it is far from commonplace. Though we represent two different branches of Judaism, these branches are nonetheless both progressive, and both seek to give women full equality in the synagogue and in the community.

There are two voices in this essay, those of father and of daughter.

The elder Rabbi Kreitman notes:
I have taken seriously the words and admonitions of the "Shema" prayer, "And you shall teach your children (literally, sons)." Within the Conservative/Masorti movement, and certainly in the Reform movement, this admonition includes daughters, even to the extent of helping them reach the height of ordination as rabbis. I have taught my daughters well and have given them a feeling of excitement about Judaism and its message. My older daughter, Jamie, went on to study the wide range of Middle Eastern languages and cultures, and she became proficient in Judeo-Arabic. Later on, she changed her focus and became a successful fashion designer. I rejoice in her many accomplishments. My younger daughter, Jill, started out as an investment banker, but soon enrolled in Hebrew Union College and was ordained as a rabbi. I am proud of her achievements as a rabbi ministering to many people, guiding them, and bringing them closer to our faith and its tradition.

The younger Rabbi Kreitman writes:
Growing up, I learned that human beings have reflexes. Some are natural, some are idle gestures, and others are reflexes of the heart. The greatest lesson my father taught me was to act on the reflex of the heart. I learned this lesson through his example. Reflexes of the heart, such as *tzedakah*,

sharing his knowledge with me in the study of Torah, Mishnah, and Talmud, and the act of building Jewish communities in America, Israel, and other lands of Jewish settlement. He loves the pulpit, it is his domain. He became one of the preeminent preachers in this country.

"Avi Mori,"–"My father, my teacher." Every moment he demonstrated that healing the world is in our hands and that giving a piece of oneself to others is a way we can touch eternity. As a little girl, I would watch my father hold the Torah lovingly in his arms. Recently, I brought my daughters, Sydney and Talia, to see their grandpa in the synagogue. It was during Rosh Hashanah services, and my father, with the Torah, was proceeding to the sacred ark, when his granddaughters rushed to his side to kiss the Torah and then to honor their grandpa.

And, again, the father shares his voice:
In teaching my daughters the texts of Judaism, I placed special emphasis on the Mishnah. It is the core of our Talmudic, rabbinic tradition, and through its study, we behold the vitality and dynamism of Jewish teaching and law. Even at moments of great stress, my daughters would join with me in the study of the Mishnah. Its words would give us strength to overcome the difficulties we encountered.

In the photograph, Jill and I are reviewing and restudying the Mishnaic tractate of Ketubot, which deals with prenuptial agreements. This document, the Ketubah, that is now part of the traditional Jewish wedding ceremony, guards the integrity and independence of the Jewish woman, and thereby upholds her sanctity. As we savored the words and arguments of Rabban Gamliel and Rabbi Joshua, who insisted on protecting the Jewish woman's independence and integrity, Jill turned to me and remarked, "It is amazing how relevant this is at this very moment."

YEHUDA KRINSKY

International Director, Chabad-Lubavitch

Rabbi Krinsky is the head of Chabad-Lubavitch, whose emissaries have brought Judaism to the four corners of the globe and to neighborhood corners around the U.S. He assumed leadership of Chabad after the death of the much-loved Rebbe, Menachem Schneerson.

"I can't say if I was successful or if I helped people; I can only say I helped the Rebbe help people, no matter if they had a life problem, or a health problem, or a business or financial matter."

I was born in Boston in 1933, into a religious family. My father was a *shochet* (meat slaughterer), and I was the youngest of nine children. In the early years there wasn't much happening in terms of Jewish education in Boston. There were Hebrew schools, but there wasn't a religious atmosphere; the education was on a secular level, even though the subject matter was Jewish. Whatever Judaism was conveyed to us as children, it was at home, by our very loving father and mother.

But without a thorough education in the proper atmosphere, my parents feared that my Jewishness would not be long-lasting. By the time I was twelve, I had a good secular background, and I was accepted into the Boston Latin School. My parents, though, were concerned not only with teaching me how to make a living, they wanted to teach me how to live. So they suggested that I transfer my records to New York, to Brooklyn, to a Lubavitch school. My maternal grandfather was a Lubavitcher Hasid, so there was a connection to Lubavitch in my family.

The people at Boston Latin couldn't understand why I was leaving this wonderful Harvard preparatory school for this unheard-of boarding school in Brooklyn. But it made no difference—my parents wanted me to go, and I wanted to go.

I came here in 1946. I would go to the Lubavitch headquarters almost every evening and on Shabbat and holidays, and I became immediately enamored with the Rebbe, who at that time was Rabbi Yosef Yitzchak Schneerson, of blessed memory. He just captured my imagination in every single way. I, along with the members of my little group of preteenagers in our bar mitzvah year, would observe him very carefully. We knew that he was a genius and an extraordinary Torah scholar, and that he was very special. Every move was weighed and pondered by this group of kids. I was drawn like a magnet to him.

Then in 1950, the Rebbe passed away and his son-in-law, Menachem Mendel Schneerson, succeeded him. It was a very difficult time, not too long after the Holocaust. But the Rebbe showered a lot of kindness on us, particularly us youngsters, and the bond just grew stronger and closer and deeper.

In 1957, just after I was married, the Rebbe's chief of staff sought me out: I had volunteered to spend the summer visiting communities around the world, meeting Jews in the streets, meeting rabbis, leaders, educators. He asked me what I planned to do for the rest of my life, what kind of a livelihood was I planning for. I told him I had no plans; I was ordained as a rabbi, but I had always been a student. He said, how would you like to become part of the Rebbe's secretariat? I couldn't refuse, because of my adoration of the Rebbe.

Soon I was involved in everything that happened in the Rebbe's office, which was the whole kaleidoscope of Jewish life, both geographically and in terms of individuals and communities.

There is a conventional understanding of what being a rabbi is—you have a synagogue, you have a congregation, what people call, "he marries and he buries." This was not the type of work that I did. I was literally assisting the Rebbe and working for the Rebbe in all the things he was involved in. I had the privilege of being in the vortex of this whole thing.

I hope I've made a contribution over the years. I'm still doing the same things that I did on the first day I came into the Rebbe's office back in 1957. I can't say if I was successful or if I helped people; I can only say I helped the Rebbe help people, no matter if they had a life problem, or a health problem, or a business or financial matter. I felt connected to the entire world's Jewish community.

Once the Rebbe was meeting with his chief of staff, who had come to him to report on the day's activities. The chief of staff said, "I have one more small matter that I want to discuss." And the Rebbe said in Yiddish, "There is no such thing as a small matter." Every individual is important and precious—that's what the Rebbe taught us. The greatest challenge we have today, after the Rebbe's passing, is to maintain this legacy, maintain this momentum. This is what keeps me afloat. It keeps me animated.

HAROLD KUSHNER
Author; Rabbi Laureate of Temple Israel, Natick, Mass.

Rabbi Harold Kushner impacted the lives of more than four million people around the word who read *When Bad Things Happen to Good People.* He has authored several other books, including *Living a Life That Matters: Resolving the Conflict Between Conscience and Success.*

"I came to the conclusion that God's promise was never that life would be fair. God's promise was that, when life was unfair, we would not have to face the unfairness alone 'for Thou art with me.'"

W hy did I become a rabbi? Do we ever understand why we make the major life decisions we do? The people we marry? The homes we are drawn to live in? The professions we choose? I became a rabbi for several reasons, some of which I understand.

My Jewish identity was an important part of who I was when I was young, and the idea of doing something that would help Judaism and the Jewish people and at the same time make an observant Jewish life possible appealed to me. I admired my rabbi, Israel Levinthal of the Brooklyn Jewish Center, and I appreciated the way he was admired by his congregation. Several of my closest friends at college were contemplating the rabbinate, and as we discussed theological and career issues, I could see myself doing what rabbis did (or what I thought rabbis did; I had seen my rabbi conduct services and give sermons, but had never seen him counseling troubled congregants or arguing for teachers' salaries at a board meeting).

But looking back, I suspect that I was attracted to the rabbinate in part as a way of following in my father's footsteps without competing with him. My father was a successful businessman and an officer of our synagogue. I knew I had no head for business, but by choosing a career in service to the Jewish people, I would be affirming the values he had lived by without having to go into business and either risk failure or risk outdoing him.

I graduated from Columbia University in 1955 and entered the rabbinical school of the Jewish Theological Seminary the following September. I immersed myself in the rabbinical school curriculum for three years, spent a year in Israel studying Bible and Talmud at the Hebrew University, spent a year of independent study concentrating on Bible, and was ordained in 1960. Though I was drawn academically to the study of Bible, and would earn a doctorate in it in 1972 for my dissertation on the history of the Book of Psalms, the teacher who influenced me most was Mordecai Kaplan and his theories of Reconstructionism. Ours was one of the last classes Dr. Kaplan taught. He was approaching his eightieth birthday when we graduated and would live to the age of 102.

In the beginning, my approach to the rabbinate was a highly cerebral, intellectual one, probably due to the fact that both of my parents (and Dr. Kaplan) had been born in Lithuania, where Judaism was generally seen as engaging the mind more than the soul. That changed in 1966 when my wife and I learned that our son Aaron suffered from the extremely rare growth disorder progeria, the rapid-aging syndrome that would cause his death in his early teens. Rational, intellectual explanations, theology that strove to justify God and ignore my pain, were of no use to me. I learned that religion had to offer consolation before it could offer explanations. I came to the conclusion that God's promise was never that life would be fair. God's promise was that, when life was unfair, we would not have to face the unfairness alone "for Thou art with me."

I was a congregational rabbi for twenty-one years in three settings: an Army chaplain in Oklahoma, assistant to Mordecai Waxman in Great Neck, Long Island, and then at Temple Israel in the Boston suburb of Natick. Then in 1981, four years after Aaron's death, I wrote a little book, *When Bad Things Happen to Good People*, telling Aaron's story and relating how I had come to understand God's role in a world where innocent people suffer. To my astonishment, it became a major best seller and has remained one ever since. I was in demand as a speaker at hundreds of churches, synagogues and medical conferences. To accommodate those demands, I cut back to part time in my congregation, and after several years, came to realize that being a congregational rabbi is not something one can do on a part-time basis. I reluctantly left the pulpit in 1990 and have been writing and lecturing since.

I feel that what I am doing now is very much an extension of my rabbinic calling, teaching from Jewish sources and bringing a message of religious consolation and healing to Jewish and non-Jewish audiences. My wife and I still live in Natick, in the same house we lived in when I was the community's rabbi.

LAWRENCE KUSHNER

Rabbi-in-Residence at Hebrew Union College-Jewish Institute of Religion, New York City; author; lecturer

Author of popular books on Jewish spirituality, as *God Was in This Place, and I, I Did Not Know*, Rabbi Kushner is among the most well-known expositors of Jewish mysticism and Kabbalah. And with a daughter who is a rabbi, he has passed on his profession and love of his religion to the next generation.

"So I put on my rabbi suit, drove into Boston, found MGH, and walked into the room. One of Boston's great physicians was just concluding a counseling session with her He motioned kindly for me to take a chair and listen in."

My first official task as the rabbi of my own congregation took me to the hospital. We had just moved into a one-bedroom apartment in Marlborough, Mass. It must have been late July. I dutifully called the president to inform him of our arrival. He welcomed me and, in the course of our conversation, said that he had heard on the grapevine that a member of the congregation was in Mass. General Hospital. She was a young mother whom he had heard was terminally ill.

So I put on my rabbi suit, drove into Boston, found MGH, and walked into the room. One of Boston's great physicians was just concluding a counseling session with her. He motioned kindly for me to take a chair and listen in.

The woman said, "But how can I be a mother? I can't even get out of bed any more."

To my astonishment, he only scolded her. "Is that what you have to do to be a mother?" he asked. "Is a mother just cooking and chauffeuring and playing?"

"No, I guess not," she whispered. "A mother is supposed to love and to teach."

"So, nu?" he replied. "Be a mother. Maybe you want to teach them about faith and about courage. Maybe you have an opportunity to love and to teach few mothers will ever understand."

She wept. He wept. I wept. "Thank you, doctor," she said. He kissed her, nodded to me, and left. I sat motionless, astonished, dumbfounded in the corner.

Startled, she turned to me and said, "Who the hell are you?"

"I'm your new rabbi," I managed to squeak. "My name is Larry Kushner."

My wife, Karen, says this is just an alternate ending for the Book of Job, where God speaks to Job from out of the whirlwind, demanding, "Where were you when I laid the foundations of the earth? Speak up, I can't hear you."

NORMAN LAMM

President, Yeshiva University, New York City

As outgoing head of Yeshiva University, the seminary that ordains the vast majority of modern Orthodox rabbis, Rabbi Lamm has had a huge influence on the leadership of traditional Judaism. He has authored several books, including his two-volume *Seventy Faces: Articles of Faith.*

"My mother's father, and his ancestors before him, for generations and generations, were rabbanim, rabbis, and it never occurred to me to exclude the rabbinate from my future."

As a young man, I struggled with my choice of career. Was it to be chemistry or the rabbinate? Psychiatry or the rabbinate? Law or the rabbinate? Cartooning or the rabbinate? The only constant in all my deliberations was the rabbinate.

Indeed, the rabbinate was on my blood–or perhaps in my genes. My mother's father, and his ancestors before him, for generations and generations, were *rabbanim*, rabbis, and it never occurred to me to exclude the rabbinate from my future. But more than genetics, it was intellectually attractive and theologically necessary. My life was drawn to Torah, even though other disciplines beckoned as well. I knew all the disadvantages of this particular calling from witnessing my grandfather, my uncle, and my great-uncle, rabbis all. But whatever drawbacks I perceived were easily outweighed by the nobility of life as a *rav* and the opportunity to study Torah and apply it to life.

So it was that I spent twenty-five years as a pulpit rabbi, and I am now in my twenty-sixth year as president of Yeshiva University. Despite Yeshiva's strong "secular" schools and programs–both undergraduate and graduate–being part of the university meant I had a large and complex "congregation" composed of believers and unbelievers, Jews and Gentiles, Orthodox and non-Orthodox. To a large extent, I transferred the skills I learned as pulpit rabbi to my responsibilities at Yeshiva University. Of course, there were many other challenges that I had to master and many more skills to learn–and perhaps some things to unlearn, as well–but I was able to practice on a much larger scale the art of being a "people person," how to communicate effectively and "sell" ideas and educational opportunities.

In the earliest years of my rabbinate, in Springfield, Mass., I learned a great deal from the people I worked with. For a New Yorker, "out of town" meant anyplace west of the Hudson River, and it took a great deal of adjustment to grow comfortable in my new position. I recall the first encounter I had with a Jew who really knew almost nothing about Judaism or rabbis. I was introduced to this estimable gentleman as the new Orthodox rabbi in town. His immediate reaction was, "You're Orthodox–and so young?" My reply was, "Sir, Orthodoxy is not a gerontological disease."

Much has happened since then. Rabbis, even traditional ones, were acculturated, and young rabbis appeared on the scene–many of whom accomplished worlds. Much more needs to be done to heal the communal sicknesses that plague us and seem unredeemable, even fatal–to all except *real* rabbis who never give up, who are reconciled to Herculean efforts, even if they yield only modest results. The effort itself is ennobling and makes all the difficulties of genuine spiritual leadership worth all the frustrations and disappointments that seem indigenous to the profession. Why? Because the rabbinate is not solely a "profession"; it is, much more accurately, a "calling," a vision, a destiny.

It was, and is, all worthwhile.

BEREL LAZAR
Chief Rabbi of Russia

Rabbi Lazar, the Chief Rabbi of Russia, met in February 2002 with Russian President Vladimir Putin to discuss important issues of Russian Jewry, including Russian Jewish emigration, the return of synagogue buildings to Jewish communities, and the relationship between Russian Jews and other communities throughout the world.

"I had the freedom to practice as a Jew in Europe, and I always had a strong desire and yearning to reach out to Soviet Jewry and teach them the Judaism and Torah of which they were being deprived."

A s a child growing up in Milan—where my parents were sent to serve the Jewish Community as emissaries of the Lubavitcher Rebbe to rebuild the community there after the war—I was always very interested and touched when I heard stories concerning the situation of the Jews in the Soviet Union. I had the freedom to practice as a Jew in Europe, and I always had a strong desire and yearning to reach out to Soviet Jewry and teach them the Judaism and Torah of which they were being deprived.

When the politics of *Perestoika* and *Glastnost* were first implemented by Mikhail Gorbachev in 1987, heralding the end of the Soviet era, I was a rabbinical student in the central Lubavitch Yeshiva in New York. I was asked to take part in a student exchange program in which I would be traveling to Russia to teach Talmud and Hassidism to Russian Jews. I was very excited about the offer, and after receiving the consent and blessing of the Lubavitcher Rebbe, I traveled to Russia. My whole trip was listed as being officially for tourist purposes, so I had to disguise myself and behave like a tourist. It didn't take long for the customs officials at the Sheremietvo airport in Moscow to figure out the real intention of my visit. They threatened that I wouldn't be let out of the country unless I was still carrying every Jewish book I brought in, to ensure that I didn't leave any with the local Jews.

Once I started meeting the Jewish activists, refuseniks, and Lubavitch Hassidim, I was in awe; in all of the stories that I had heard, their heroism was understated. They risked their jobs and put their families in danger to observe even simple *mitzvot* (commandments). Doing anything Jewish—even being part of this underground community—was very dangerous, but they carried out their work as if it was everyday routine. When I was being followed by the KGB, I was constantly filled with fear of being caught.

Right before my departure I pledged to those people I met that if the possibility arose, I would return to Russia permanently to help. After I got married the situation in Russia began to change, with the fall of Communism. My wife and I were sent back to Russia by the Rebbe to help rebuild the Jewish community.

Arriving in Russia, I was appointed rabbi of the Marina Rodsha synagogue, one of the two synagogues that remained in operation throughout the years of communism. Besides teaching, I knew we would need to rebuild the structure of the Jewish community. Our first task was to restore Jewish education. In 1989, we opened the first Jewish day school in Moscow; we had only seventeen students. Through the Herculean efforts of the emissaries of Lubavitcher Rabbis across the former Soviet Union, this tiny knot of dedicated students expanded beyond anyone's expectations. Today, the Federation of Jewish Communities of the former Soviet Union oversees sixty-two Jewish educational institutions in forty-eight cities throughout the former Soviet Union, with an aggregate enrollment exceeding 12,000 students.

During the past twelve years, I have met many dignitaries and government officials. One of the meetings I will never forget was with Boris Yeltsin. At that time, he pledged to work on a law that would enable the Jewish community to receive its religious buildings back from the government. (The buildings had been confiscated under the Soviets.) I was extremely impressed by his knowledge of Jewish issues and the history of the Jewish people in Russia.

One of the most terrifying moments I remember was the night the Marina Rodsha Synagogue burned down. We soon rebuilt a temporary structure—and that was bombed. We rounded up the community, and in the face of daunting odds and widespread fear, we vowed to rebuild the defiant little shul that survived the Communist regime. As a fulfillment of this promise, I—together with the Chief Rabbi of Israel, Israel Meir Lau, and the mayor of Moscow, Yuri Luzhkov—laid the groundbreaking stone in Aug. 1994 for a seven-story Jewish Community Center and Synagogue on the site of the bombed-out synagogue. In Sept. 2000, our vision came to fruition with the inauguration of the Center in a ceremony that featured the Russian President Vladimir Putin. It was a symbol of how much had changed for the Jews of Russia in the years I have worked with them.

WILLIAM LEBEAU

Vice Chancellor for Rabbinic Development, Jewish Theological Seminary, New York City

Rabbi Lebeau is the Vice Chancellor for Rabbinic Development at the Jewish Theological Seminary. He also served as Dean of the Rabbinical School for six years. Rabbi Lebeau was a Chaplain in the U.S. Navy, and was the congregational rabbi in Port Jefferson Station, N.Y., and Highland Park, Ill. He is married and has five children and five grandchildren.

"'Mr. Lebeau,' he countered, 'as a rabbi, you must learn to feel God's presence everywhere–even in the most mundane and trying of circumstances.' It's a lesson I've never forgotten."

S hortly after my bar mitzvah, Rabbi Norman Shapiro came to Akron's Beth-El Congregation as spiritual leader. He inspired me to study Jewish texts on a serious level, and when I showed interest, he encouraged me to complete my last two years of college in New York City, where I could take courses at the Jewish Theological Seminary. I attended New York University. In the evening, I would come uptown to take classes at the Seminary College (today the Albert A. List College of JTS). I fell in love with the study of Jewish texts.

Through study, I was drawn to make a deeper commitment to Jewish observance, and that was the first step on the road to becoming a rabbi. Another step was my realization that the rabbinate would allow me to address the future of the Jewish people, which was of profound concern to me.

Still, I was plagued by doubts. In fact, initially I dismissed the notion. How could I even think it appropriate to envision myself as a member of the select association of rabbis respected for their piety and knowledge? I could not understand how others made the passage into the rabbinate. They clearly possessed the qualities that earned them recognition as "Rabbi." I had lived the first nineteen years of my life without a working relationship with God. I was far beyond the boundaries of traditional Jewish life. It was presumptuous for me to think that I might become a rabbi with my vague notion of wanting to help preserve the Jewish people.

One day I heard the rabbi and cantor of my congregation referred to as *k'lai kodesh* (vessels of holiness). The strange description helped me consider the possibility that I could acquire the qualifications for the rabbinate. Thinking of the rabbi and cantor of my synagogue as *k'lai kodesh* allowed me to think of them as instruments for transmitting the sacredness of the Jewish tradition to others rather than as holy men set aside from others. I understood that they were not born with attributes spontaneously qualifying them for religious leadership. Instead, they developed in ways that prepared them for the rabbinate.

My interview for admission to rabbinical school stands out in my memory. I was very nervous. Among those around the table was the renowned scholar Rabbi Abraham Joshua Heschel. "Mr. Lebeau," he asked, "did you see God today?" I thought about how I had been rushing to get to JTS that morning, walking from my apartment focused on getting to the interview on time. I tried to parry the question. "I've seen God on a beautiful day in the park, in the flowers and trees and the smiling faces of children," I responded.

But he persisted. "I asked if you saw God today." "No," I was forced to admit. "I was distracted by my meeting with this committee. I don't believe I saw God today." "Mr. Lebeau," he countered, "as a rabbi, you must learn to feel God's presence everywhere–even in the most mundane and trying of circumstances." It's a lesson I've never forgotten. I have responded since that moment to Rabbi Heschel's challenge to search for God in every dimension of my life experience.

Following my ordination, I spent two years in San Diego as a chaplain at the U.S. Naval Recruitment Training Center and the Marine Recruitment Center. My chaplaincy began only days after the beginning of the Vietnam War. I was responsible for one thousand Jewish draftees, many as young as seventeen and away from home for the first time. They were facing combat and potentially death.

When I took my first pulpit, at the North Shore Jewish Center in Port Jefferson, Long Island, there were sixty families in the congregation. When I left thirteen years later, we had grown to 750 families. It was a gift being the rabbi of a congregation that grew so dramatically. I loved working with the school, the children, and young families as our own five children were growing up. I felt as if we were part of a big extended family, growing in our love of Judaism together. Next, I became spiritual leader for the following decade at North Suburban Synagogue Beth El, in Highland Park, Illinois. What I loved most about being a congregational rabbi was being able to devote every day to what I feel most passionate about: Judaism's teachings and the Jewish people.

MAYA LEIBOVICH

Kehilat Mevasseret Zion, Israel; first Israeli-born woman ordained in Israel

Born in Ramat Gan, Israel, Rabbi Leibovich is the first Israeli-born woman ordained by the Hebrew Union College in Jerusalem. She is the rabbi of Kehilat Mevasseret Zion and is coeditor of *Baruch Sh'Assani Isha and Gog u'magog*, both published by Yediot Acharonot. She has four children.

"As a child I was always in dialogue with the forbidden God and I was curious to have a family saga of my own."

The rabbinate has filled my life. Being a daughter of two Holocaust survivors I was raised with a gap in my family history. What happened back there in Czechoslovakia was that of which we never spoke, nor were we allowed to ask questions. There were no grandparents or uncles or aunts to fill me or my brother in on the story of the past. When I grew up and it was popular to take "Roots Journeys" with your family, trips tracing familial history in the "old country," my parents were not ready to set foot on that land. Along with the lost past, our family lost all contact with Jewish tradition. My father was so angry with God that it was a struggle to convince him to hold a Seder on Passover.

I was raised on the ethos of the new Sabra (Israeli native), so different from the Galut (Diaspora) Jew, as my parents understood it. As a child I was always in dialogue with the forbidden God and I was curious to have a family saga of my own.

The rabbinate allowed me a journey back into the past. It gave me the tools to not only search through letters and documents, but to rummage and tackle ideas and beliefs and values that my people held to. The rabbinate taught me to be a knowledgeable, as well as a conscientious, Jew.

During my years of study for the rabbinate, I also finished my research on the history of my family, and now they are all part of the archives at Yad Vashem, Israel's Holocaust museum and research center.

My rediscovered Jewish identity has made me a more whole human being. I have chosen the rabbinate and not an academic field, because as a rabbi, I have a duty to pass on that which I have learned, and my family life is so much richer because of this duty. I hope my congregation's life is so much richer too.

LEE LEVINE

Dean, Hebrew University-Institute of Archeology, Jerusalem

Rabbi Levine is Professor of Jewish history and archeology at Hebrew University. He founded the first TALI school in Jerusalem, to which there are now 105 Tali programs throughout Israel. He has just finished a book about the history of Jerusalem during the Second Temple period. He has four children and four grandchildren.

"My academic work has focused on several areas, each of which has allowed me to integrate the historical and literary data with that derived from archeological excavations."

T he most formative Jewish experience in my youth were the thirteen summers I spent at Camp Ramah, which is affiliated with the Conservative Movement. It allowed me not only to immerse myself in an intensive Jewish experience for eight weeks each summer, but also to befriend a group of exceptionally dedicated people, many of whom would remain my closest friends for life. Those summers certainly were crucial in sparking and maintaining my interest in Judaism, so much so that when it came time to choose a college, I found myself at Columbia because of its proximity to the Jewish Theological Seminary (JTS) in New York. During college, my wife-to-be, Mira, and I came to Israel for a year of study; although we both had a stimulating and rich experience, we never considered aliyah seriously at that point; we both saw ourselves as serving the American Jewish community.

After college, I continued my studies in the JTS rabbinical program, but influenced by several teachers, especially the future chancellor of the institution, Gerson Cohen, I decided to shift professional goals from serving as a congregational rabbi to an academic track at JTS. Concomitantly, I pursued an M.A. and doctorate at Columbia University in the fields of Jewish and ancient history. My Ph.D. thesis, on Caesarea under Roman Rule, proved to be a fateful choice. My advisors urged me to spend a year in Israel in order to study the archeological material related to the topic, and it was then that Professor Y. Yadin invited me to join the faculty of Hebrew University. We agreed to come only after having completed our studies in New York, and thus we made aliyah in 1971. I have taught in the University's archaeology and Jewish history departments since then.

My academic work has focused on several areas, each of which has allowed me to integrate the historical and literary data with that derived from archeological excavations. Thus, for example, one area of concentration has been the study of ancient synagogues. I was astounded upon arrival in Israel by how much material was accumulating about ancient synagogues each year, and by the central place that the institution played in Jewish life of antiquity.

I was also given the opportunity to introduce a different conception of Judaism to the Israeli scene, where the vast majority of synagogues are Orthodox. In 1973, many of our friends from Ramah and JTS made their homes in the French Hill neighborhood in Jerusalem, and we were among the founding members of a Conservative synagogue, Ramot Zion. Our synagogue provides an appealing alternative to Israelis in search of their Jewish roots, both for those who were born Orthodox and for those who grew up in secular homes.

Not long thereafter, many of us began talking about starting a new kind of public school. There has existed here in Israel a fairly rigid dichotomy between the general, secular public schools and the Orthodox public schools. We sought to create a new kind of school that would integrate the best of both: an open, pluralistic, tolerant atmosphere where secular studies are seriously engaged as well as affording intensive exposure to Jewish tradition on both the cognitive and experiential levels. We started the first such TALI (a Hebrew acronym for Enriched Jewish Studies) school in 1976 on French Hill with thirty-three pupils. Today there are some 15,000 students in Tali programs in Israel.

It was also my privilege to be involved in establishing the Seminary of Jewish Studies in 1984 (today renamed the Schechter Institute for Jewish Studies), an institution aiming to train rabbis and educators for Israel's Masorti (Conservative) Movement. Beginnings can often be difficult, and so it was in this case. Thus after three years, in 1987, I was asked to head the Seminary, which I did until 1994. During that time, we developed the rabbinical and educational programs, and opened a flourishing academic program in Jewish studies that was connected with JTS. In addition, an adult education for Israelis was created, as well as programs and institutions to serve Diaspora communities, particularly those in the former Soviet Union. When I started out we had only nine students; when I left it had reached 350. An exciting period in my life was accompanied by the pride of having helped to create an institution that is filling a vital role in Jewish society.

DOVID MENACHEM MENDEL LIEBERSOHN

Chabad Lubavitch, Barcelona, Spain

A Chabad rabbi in Barcelona, Rabbi Liebersohn is among the emissaries sent by Chabad-Lubavitch to bring Judaism around the Earth.

"I'm sure everyone who was at the first seder will never forget it. People were singing and dancing. All the children started to sing Ani Maamin, a song about our belief in the coming of the Messiah."

I don't remember the day I decided to be a *rov* (rabbi). The truth is that my father is a rov and my grandfather was a *rov* too, but I don't think that this is what made me a rov, because more than a rov, I'm a *schliach*– emissary. This is a word that unifies thousands of rabbis in the world; we are all *schluchim*, emissaries of one man, our beloved rebbe, the Lubavitcher Rebbe.

The Rebbe taught us that our goal is to fill the life of each Jew with a little bit more Judaism, because a little bit added to a little bit more becomes a lot of Judaism. And for this goal, it doesn't matter how many Jews there are in a city, or if the city is far or near, because every Jew is a whole world by himself.

Today, our city is Barcelona. Here we're feeling like an inseparable part of the Jewish community. Together with my wife, Nechama Dina, and our children, Chaya Mushka and Shalom Dovber– who were born in Barcelona–we are trying to enact change, to instill the responsibility for the eternity of *Am Yisroel*–the people of Israel–inside of each and every Jew. And in this way, we hope to approach these Jews and to bring them to Torah and *mitzvos* (commandments).

Today, after three years of work, it's amazing to think about the first steps we made in this city. Everything started when I first came to visit this community on a summer program, part of the Lubavitch program of Jewish community enrichment. Our goal was to present the directors of the Jewish community with a proposition aimed at inciting them to do more activity related to Jewish observance, to instill in their consciences the idea that the priority of a community needs to be the study of Torah and maintaining the legacy of Judaism. Those initial efforts bore fruit, and the community decided it wanted a Chabad rabbi.

During our first Passover here, every face was new and getting to know every Jew in this city was a special experience. We moved into our apartment a month before Passover, but we decided to stay and make Passover in our apartment–rather than going elsewhere, where it would be easier–because we wanted and needed to make a difference in Barcelona that very Passover.

A week before Passover began, we received our oven. Two young Lubavitch boys came from New York to help us. When we started to get ready for the holiday, the phone didn't stop ringing. People wanted to know if they could join us for the seder. We were expecting thirty people for the second seder, plus another forty guests that would come by during the holiday to join us for other Passover meals.

It was only when my wife started cooking that she realized the work that was expected of her: She made three hundred pieces of gefilte fish from scratch, grinding the fish and molding the balls. The matzah and the wine was brought from Israel. We ordered a container of chickens from France, and we waited for it until the day before Passover, when we received a phone call telling us the container was lost. My wife was in her ninth month of pregnancy and busy preparing so much food for Passover–and now she had to manage without chickens. But she made kugels, and used a lot of fish and eggs, and thank G-d, she managed.

I'm sure everyone who was at the first seder will never forget it. People were singing and dancing. All the children started to sing "Ani Maamin", a song about our belief in the coming of the Messiah. The seder finished at 2 a.m. with everyone in high spirits. Everyone there felt happy to be a Jew.

The second seder also was unbelievable. The Rebbe gave us strength and blessing. A lady who came from Miami told us, with tears in her eyes, "Usually, Passover is spent with family, but this year we are with a big family." We were thirty people around our table, and we explained the Haggada in different languages. Everyone who came into our home saw our big picture of the Rebbe and asked who he was. We explained that it was the Rebbe who sent us to Barcelona, and that there are thousands of other emissaries like us around the world. This made them feel very close to the Rebbe.

SHLOMO MAIDANCHIK

President, Agudath Chasidai

A former locomotive engineer, Rabbi Maidanchik today is chairman of Chabad in Israel.

"Just seeing a train engineer with the beard and look of a Hasidic Jew was an inspiring novelty, and I always had a pair of tefillin with me for the workers, conductors, and passengers to use."

In my youth, I was not at all religious, but was a faithful and zealous member of a communist youth movement in the Ukraine, which was then, of course, part of the Soviet Union. With the outbreak of war, my family began to move from the front, and while we were in Tashkent in 1941, I became acquainted with Chabad Lubavitch Hasidim and started to become observant.

After the war, I became a railroad engineer, and in 1949 my family fled through Europe to Israel to escape Stalinist oppression. In Israel, we found rampant unemployment, but I soon found job as a railroad engineer. The manager—a secular Zionist hostile to observant Jews—said to me, "You may be a genius in trains, but here we work on Shabbat, and you are going to work on Shabbat." I replied, "I left Russia because I refused to work on Shabbat. If Stalin couldn't make me work, you are certainly not going to."

Soon after, I settled in Kfar Chabad and was elected mayor of the town. The Rebbe soon gave me another responsibility: He appointed me the representative of Chabad to the government and the army. I got to know all the prime ministers and many Knesset members and generals. I would bring them matzah before Passover, invite them to every official Chabad function, and try to convince them to obey as many commandments as possible.

But the Rebbe would never consent for me to cease work as an engineer. He discouraged me from taking a higher position that would have taken me away from the throttle and put me behind a desk. I was able to spread Judaism through my position. Just seeing a train engineer with the beard and look of a Hasidic Jew was an inspiring novelty, and I always had a pair of tefillin with me for the workers, conductors, and passengers to use.

Once there was a bomb found on the tracks. While we were waiting for it to be diffused, I went from passenger to passenger offering them to put on the tefillin. One man asked me how long it would be before we got moving again. I replied, "We aren't going anywhere until you put on tefillin." Somehow, he believed me, put them on, and when he was finished, the police announced we could resume the trip.

All the time, I have felt that I have been purely at the service of the Rebbe. I, of course, am very human, with many faults, but the other workers have always treated me like an angel. I look forward to the coming of *Moshiach*—the Messiah—and it is up to us to bring him as soon as possible.

DOW MARMUR
Interim Executive Director, World Union for Progressive Judaism

MICHAEL MARMUR
Dean, Hebrew Union College-Jewish Institute of Religion, Jerusalem

Rabbi Dow Marmur was born in Poland, grew up in Sweden, and was ordained in 1962 by the Leo Baeck College in London. He is Rabbi Emeritus, Holy Blossom Temple, Toronto, and is the author of numerous books and articles.

Born in Britain, Rabbi Michael Marmur came to Israel in 1984. He is responsible for training rabbis from North America and Israel.

"I am in a family business. My father, with whom I am pictured here, is my confidant, best friend, and professional role model."

Dow Marmur

Looking back on my career and remembering how I embarked on it, I have come to understand why I chose to be a rabbi in the first place. Most of the children of the generation of Polish Jews to which my wife Fredzia and I belong were wiped out by the Holocaust. In one way or another, we have asked ourselves why we survived. Of course, there is no answer. But in our perplexity, we wanted to vindicate our survival. Serving the Jewish people became our way of proving to ourselves that we were saved for a purpose.

Emil Fackenheim, the eminent Jewish thinker, has written that, after the Holocaust, Jews must obey an additional commandment: not to give Hitler a posthumous victory. Surviving as Jews and making sure that Jews thrive and Judaism flourishes is the way in which we, as survivors, can find meaning in our existence. I think that that's why I, who lived through World War II in various parts of the Soviet Union, became a rabbi, and why my life partner, a survivor of the Lodz ghetto and the concentration camp of Ravensbrueck, encouraged me, and throughout my ministry, came to share in my work.

Having children and bringing them up as Jews was another dimension of the commandment Fackenheim formulated. Our two daughters and son, their spouses and their children have turned us into a family determined to keep Judaism alive. The fact that our son is a rabbi in Israel and that three of our grandchildren live there further strengthens this determination.

In part, I have my wife to thank for the fact that I am a rabbi at all. Fredzia Zonabend survived World War II as a child and came to live in Stockholm. We met at a conference for Jewish youth in Scandinavia, and though we were still in our teens, we decided that it was *bashert*–a match made in heaven. I told Fredzia of my plans to become a rabbi. She was most encouraging and has been by my side ever since.

My commitment to Reform Judaism and to Zionism is a manifestation of my belief in the future. Among the various positions I have held, I am particularly proud to have been the founding chairman of Arzenu, the international organization of Reform Zionists. The continuity of the Jewish people remains problematic, both in the Diaspora and in Israel. I pray for more years of active work and new challenges that will help me to continue to vindicate my choice of vocation.

Michael Marmur

I am told that when I was a small child, after my bath I would wrap the towel around myself like a prayer shawl and deliver sermons to whomever was around to listen.

I am in a family business. My father, with whom I am pictured here, is my confidant, best friend, and professional role model. That kind of proximity can sometimes be problematic, but he and I have solved a lot of the potential complications by having lived on different continents for most of my adult life. By having trained for the rabbinate and worked as a rabbi in Israel, I have managed to emulate my father's professional example without ever trying to duplicate it.

To be a rabbi is to act as a bridge between an ancient tradition and a contemporary reality. In a sense we represent this tradition, or aspects of it, as the Jews we serve struggle to survive and flourish in a complicated world. And we also represent these Jews before the court of Jewish tradition. We ask that tradition: Do you have a way of understanding and including these Jews, just as we ask our congregants, "Are you prepared to hear the voice of this tradition?" And as a Reform rabbi, I have to remind myself and others that this tradition is neither homogeneous nor static. It has many faces, it is sung in many voices.

ROLANDO MATALON & MARCELO BRONSTEIN

Rabbis of Congregation B'nai Jeshurun, New York City

Rabbi Matalon and Rabbi Bronstein are rabbis of Congregation B'nai Jeshrun in New York's Upper West Side, and as such are leaders of a social phenomenon. B'nai Jeshrun, or BJ, is a magnet for Gen X Jews interested in tradition, social activism, and acceptance. The congregation is welcoming to individuals and families of all beliefs, sexual orientations, and its Friday night services have become a central gathering place for young Jews.

"Being a member of B'nai Jeshurun means that we are here to serve and not to be served. We are here to deepen our Judaism so that we may better serve God."

B'nai Jeshurun's mission is to inspire and require. We seek to inspire the quest for a measure of sanctity in the midst of so much secularity, and the search for meaning in our lives.

We base the mission of B'nai Jeshurun on the words of our teacher, Rabbi Marshall T. Meyer, of blessed memory: Congregation B'nai Jeshurun believes that a community synagogue that responds to the authentic questions of life, death, love, anxiety, longing, and the search for meaning can, once again, attract Jews–families and individuals–if it is willing to grapple with the great issues of life.

What is the purpose of my existence? How do I respond as a Jew to the exigencies of life? How can I do my part to repair the world? These are some of the authentic questions of life, and wrestling with them has always been at the soul of Judaism. It is at the soul of B'nai Jeshurun today.

Our tradition teaches us that this quest for meaning does not and cannot take place alone. It must be undertaken within a community. And to have the power to change our lives, and through our lives the world, that community must be more than a group of like-minded individuals. To be truly transformative, it must be a *kehillah kedoshah*, a sacred community.

But inspiration is not enough. There must also be requirement. Without requirement, the individual cannot be enriched and the community cannot be strengthened. We ask that each member of B'nai Jeshurun commit him or herself to engaging in study that is probing and relevant, prayer with true intention, observance that is meaningful, and acts of lovingkindness that bring us closer to the repair of the world.

Being a member of B'nai Jeshurun means that we are here to serve and not to be served. We are here to deepen our Judaism so that we may better serve God.

PAUL MENITOFF
Executive Vice President, Central Conference of American Rabbis

Rabbi Menitoff (Hebrew Union College-Jewish Institute of Religion) is Executive Vice President of the Central Conference of American Rabbis (CCAR), which represents rabbis in Reform Judaism around the world.

"In an era in which our people are steeped in modernity, how do we respond in concise, cogent, and compelling terms to the question, 'Why be Jewish?'"

A s a rabbi, the following questions challenge me daily, even more so than pulling myself out of bed each morning at 5:15 a.m. for my jog:

1) In an era in which a substantial number of our young people have graduate degrees, but at best only a ninth-grade Jewish education, how can we increase their level of Jewish knowledge?

2) How can we create a reservoir of Jewish role models and memories for our children, equal to those that made being Jewish as natural as breathing for our grandparents?

3) How can we break the Orthodox monopoly on religion in Israel, and (equally important) how can we attract Israel's massive numbers of secular Jews to Reform Judaism?

4) How can we work to close the growing gap between the "haves" and "have nots," so that we can achieve *tikkun olam*–the perfection of the world–and not be consumed by terrorist and Farrakhan-like demagogues?

5) How can we focus sufficient attention and the resources of the synagogue movements, the federation system, and congregations on creating venues for young Jews to meet other young Jews?

6) In an era in which our people are steeped in modernity, how do we respond in concise, cogent, and compelling terms to the question, "Why be Jewish?"

SHALOM PALTIEL

Spiritual Leader, Congregation Chabad of Port Washington, N.Y.

Rabbi Paltiel is the Executive Director of Chabad of Port Washington, Long Island, N.Y., and Dean, Chabad Academy of Science and the Humanities.

"When I came to town, you would hardly ever see someone with a yarmulke walking down the street or a mezuzah on a storefront."

I was inspired by a great rabbi–the Lubavitcher Rebbe Menachem Mendel Schneerson–to devote my life to teaching Jewishness. Since childhood, that was my aspiration: to go out, become a rabbi, and be able to share traditional Judaism with modern Jews.

My wife and I moved in 1991 to Port Washington, on Long Island's North Shore, to establish our Chabad synagogue here. We started it from scratch, in our living room. Our dream from childhood was to go out and open a Chabad House and be able to bring Yiddishkeit to people. We found this community, which is a nice Jewish community, and we felt we could add something to the community. In the beginning, we held services in the living room of a little apartment. We grew very quickly, and before long, people were lining the hallways of the apartment. We rented some office space for services, and three years ago built a beautiful new synagogue. My wife and I formed the congregation by attracting people to it, which was beautiful; it's not like people came and said, "We want to hire you." People said "We like what you offer," and so they became part of our new community.

Some Chabad rabbis like to go to godforsaken places. We chose Port Washington because we wanted to go to a location where there was no Chabad House as of yet but where there also was a substantial number of Jews. There were few communities with substantial Jewish populations in the U.S. that did not already have Chabad Centers, so that's how we ended up here. When I came to town, you would hardly ever see someone with a yarmulke walking down the street or a mezuzah on a storefront. I remember walking around town, on Main Street, and people were not sure what I was doing there. One guy pulled over and said, "Are you lost?" Today, there has been a big change.

I remember meeting a high-powered attorney who lives in this community and who ended up becoming involved with us. He was generations away from any Jewish observance. I spoke to him in his fancy office; he seemed to be a nice guy and interested in our work. I was getting ready to leave. I always carry a pair of tefillin, in case there's an opportunity to make a *bracha*–blessing– with a fellow Jew, and in doing so, hopefully inspire them. I wanted to share this mitzvah with this attorney, but I was almost too humbled to do it in his fancy Manhattan office. I was a young rabbi, and he was a successful attorney. I finally said, "Would you like to put on tefillin?" And he said okay. We did the tefillin, and I really rushed it because he was busy. He turned to me afterward and said, "You know, rabbi, this was the most peaceful moment I had in six months." Shortly after, he called me and said he wanted me to come back. "When I spend time with you, I feel at peace," he told me. It's not because of my personality–it's because of what I represent. I am offering goods people want. People have success, they have education, they have a lot of good things, but they're looking for that inner meaning. Torah has it.

I get a big thrill out of getting to know people with very little knowledge of traditional Judaism– who have all kinds of ideas and stereotypes about Orthodoxy–and helping to change their attitudes. I constantly meet people who insist they will never step foot in an Orthodox shul. But they are my fellow Jews, my brothers and sisters. I teach them that Judaism and Torah are good, they are valuable, and that they are the greatest gift God gave us. Torah makes life wonderful and special. My life wouldn't be the same without it, and I show them what Judaism means to me. So often I later get the chance to see these same people and their families become passionately involved in Yiddishkeit. Their transformation speaks to the truth of Torah and the genuine truth in the heart of every Jew. People learn that Torah is not just dogma and that Judaism does not always conform to the stereotypes of what they think it is. Torah has a message for their lives, it makes their lives better, and they love it.

But I am not satisfied in the least at what has been accomplished. We will continue to share "Judaism with a Smile," as taught to us by our inspired Rebbe, until we have touched every Jew in our community with the warm, welcoming message of Judaism.

STEPHEN PASSAMANECK

Professor of Rabbinics, Hebrew Union College, Los Angeles; chaplain, United States Bureau of Alcohol, Tobacco, and Firearms

M y rabbinate divides neatly into two aspects. The first is study, research, and teaching. The second is law enforcement chaplaincy. The study, research, and teaching came first in terms of time, so that is where I shall begin.

Long before I had completed the rabbinical course of study at the Hebrew Union College in Cincinnati, one matter had become certain. I had no interest in serving in a pulpit, but in those days of the early 1960s, that is what most of the graduates did. Instead, the idea of further study had a greater appeal to me. So I took a fellowship and pursued a doctoral program at HUC.

Of all the possibilities in Jewish studies, the one that truly appealed to me was the legal tradition of the Talmud and the post-Talmudic masters. Jewish law was, after all, the area that had commanded the attention of the greatest minds of the rabbinate, and my hometown rabbi, Solomon B. Freehof, of blessed memory, had set a grand example in that field for the entire Reform Jewish movement. In time, I received the doctoral degree, but more importantly, I was fortunate enough to secure a position on the faculty of the Los Angeles campus of the HUC, where I have taught ever since.

Teaching Talmud and related material has always meant for me a process of continuing study; there is always more to learn. My congregants, so to speak, have been my students, scores of them over the years. There is always something exciting and refreshing about each new session of class. One never knows what questions will be asked, or what problems will be raised. The task of introducing generations of bright and eager minds to the great works of their heritage has been and remains a source of endless fascination and delight. The students–my congregants–have never ceased to surprise and gratify me over my years of teaching. But there is that second aspect of my rabbinate: law enforcement chaplaincy. This interest began in the mid-'70s, and it has ever since served to shape my scholarly interests. My first exposure to law enforcement chaplaincy came when I responded to a newspaper article describing the sort of ministry that some local clergy were providing to the Los Angeles County Sheriffs' Department. I joined and got some on-the-job training. This chaplaincy exposed me to people, places, and experiences that most rabbis never encounter. My law enforcement "congregation" was almost always non-Jewish.

Law enforcement chaplaincy brings one into contact with the hard and often tragic realities of modern life. No cameras capture the chaplain at work comforting officers and civilians at the scene of a child suicide at 3 a.m. on a rainy November morning, or comforting the family evacuated when an armed man barricades himself in the house next door. Being a chaplain offered me the opportunity to meet a non-Jewish constituency that often had no real contact with Jews, much less a rabbi. Thus there was the chance to teach and broaden the perspective of the men and women who are, after all, charged with protecting the rights and well being of us all.

In the mid-'80s I attended the Sheriffs' Reserve Academy and emerged five months later as a sworn Reserve Deputy Sheriff. I worked both patrol and detective assignments, but most of my time was spent with a plainclothes surveillance and apprehension unit. But I grew too old for that sort of work, resigned from the Sheriffs' Dept., and became a chaplain with the federal Bureau of Alcohol, Tobacco, and Firearms, where I continue to serve. Through my law enforcement ministry I have tried to be of service to both officers and civilians, from the mean streets of south L.A., to a bullet-riddled street in a quiet suburb–all the way to Ground Zero, or Ground Hero as I call it, after the World Trade Center tragedy. I will always remember my time at Ground Hero. Firefighters would come up to me and greet me with: "Howyadoin', Father?" They all thought I was a priest. One day, a grimy, exhausted man held out a religious medal and asked me to bless it; I agreed, offering a mixed Hebrew and Latin benediction.

JOSHUA PLAUT

Executive Director of the Center for Jewish History, New York City

Rabbi Plaut is a cultural anthropologist, folklorist, and widely exhibited photo-ethnographer of worldwide Jewish communities. He is a Ph.D. candidate in Judaic Studies at NYU. He is often referred to as the Vineyard Rebbe, and still has a home and lives on Martha's Vineyard, Mass.

"As a Cultural Anthropologist and Folklorist, recounting new stories born of our own time and telling sacred stories from days gone by, I both impart the historical narrative and am shaped by it."

E ach and every Jew, in each and every generation, holds the Torah in a unique way. As a rabbi, I have been able to connect Jews to their heritage, inspiring them to discover their own unique Jewish pathway. I am a teacher. I am an active transmitter of tradition. I am an emissary. I try to bring near the divine presence–to release God's holy sparks in the seemingly simple moments of each day. I am a storyteller of Jewish life, far and near. As a photo-ethnographer, I have always viewed the world through a Jewish lens and encourage fellow Jews to view life with Jewish eyes. As a cultural anthropologist and folklorist, recounting new stories born of our own time and telling sacred stories from days gone by, I both impart the historical narrative and am shaped by it.

Birth, marriage, and death–core life events–always stir me. Performing a wedding ceremony brings tears of joy to my eyes. The very moment the bride and groom enter the *chupah*, I feel joyful and yet contemplative. The bride and groom are a new link in a chain of tradition that traces back thousands of years.

Death can also be at once solemn and a joyful time for reflection. During the summer of 1994, a member of my congregation passed away. Born Thelma Vanderhoop, a Wampanoag Indian, she met Milton Weisberg on an island beach. Thelma converted to Judaism, and they married. Milton later studied to become a rabbi. Upon her death, having outlived her husband and having borne no children, Thelma's Native American nephews and nieces turned to me to plan the funeral. Despite my guidance rooted in Jewish tradition, certain Wampanoag customs seeped in. The nieces and nephews arranged *shmirah*, the guarding of Thelma's body–but in a somewhat unusual manner. The night before the funeral, Thelma rested peacefully in an open pine casket bearing a carved Jewish star. She was adorned in deerskin, her lifeless fingers clutching bird feathers and a tiny medicine pouch. At the graveside ceremony in the Jewish cemetery, after I concluded the traditional Jewish burial rites, the tribe members chanted, beat drums and leapt over the newly filled grave. Though there were no clouds in the sky and it was a month without rain, a rainbow suddenly appeared in the sky. Wampanoag tradition teaches that in the guise of a soaring eagle, the departed soul ascends above. In this case, they said Rabbi Milton was carrying his dear Thelma on the arc of the rainbow to the gates of heaven.

At times, I find myself both participating in and bearing witness to history. In September 1994, as the rabbi on the island of Martha's Vineyard, I invited President and Mrs. Clinton to attend our Rosh Hashanah services, and during services asked the president to join me on the pulpit. I blew a long blast on the shofar and challenged the president to lead us in the charge forward to a world without weapons, a world with peace upon Jerusalem. A year later, the White House invited me to attend a reception in Washington on the day that Arafat, Rabin, and Clinton signed the Oslo Two peace accords. These three leaders stood opposite me. Flanking them were President Mubarak of Egypt and King Hussein of Jordan. I photographed this historic assemblage of leaders. Rabin's words at that time were prophetic, and in retrospect, chilling. Rabin urged the audience to take a good look at the gathering of world leaders–for the future was uncertain. Two weeks later, Yitzhak Rabin was assassinated, signaling the slow demise of the peace process.

I have recorded contemporary life histories of Jews in Samarkand and Auckland, Salonika and Marrakech, Jerusalem, and New York. My emphasis has shifted to capturing the renewal of Jewish life in America. Immersed in the life of the cultures I visit, my photographs convey images of Jews and Jewish life in places that at first glance may seem unfamiliar, but reflect the thread of a shared destiny. I leave the interpretation to the viewer, knowing they will discover a familiar connection with places and people who share a portable and proud heritage. Perhaps some will even realize that each one of us is capable of holding the Torah in our own way and in our own time.

JOSEPH POTASNIK

Congregation Mount Sinai, Brooklyn, N.Y.; President of the New York Board of Rabbis

Rabbi Potasnik is Fire Chaplain for the City of New York. He is host of ABC's *Religion on the Line* and does commentaries for WINS radio.

"As a Fire Chaplain, I have tried to bring more tradition into the lives of our firefighters. They, however, have brought more life into the beauty of of our tradition."

Jewish tradition teaches, "Be holy, be holy, but above all be a mentsch–a good person." I have been privileged to serve two holy congregations comprised of mentsches from Congregation Mount Sinai and the New York City Fire Department respectively. Since September 11, 2001, I have learned that firefighters are the most religious people in society. How many individuals do we know who will run into a building to save lives while others are running out to save their lives. Mayor Rudolph Guiliani once said, "When New York's Bravest race to rescue people, they never ask, 'What is the race or religion of the person.'" Is the victim rich or poor, young or old? They recognize that we are all descendants of the first human family, and thus we are of one blood.

When we were very young and were asked what we wanted to be in later years, we would answer, "a firefighter or a policeman." Perhaps we recognized that the real heroes of life are those who try to make a difference in life. Interestingly, Jewish tradition sees life in the plural and does not write life in the singular form. As firefighters know, life only matters when shared with another soul. A famous song is entitled "I've Got to Be Me," but the firefighters proclaim, "I've Got to Be We."

The greatest spiritual challenge for me as a rabbi is facing the family of a fallen firefighter who has lost his life. I know that there are no particular words or prayers that can truly mitigate the pain of that loving family. However, I often find much sustaining strength in seeing the special closeness shared by so many members of the Department. These sacred souls truly believe they are servants of G-d in their service to humankind. Becoming a firefighter is a lifelong ambition or a family legacy that cannot be fulfilled with any other profession. The prophet proclaimed, "A person of spirit is somewhat crazy." He is someone who is not satisfied with the conventional roles of life but dares to confront the dangerous challenges of daily living. I will always remember the words of a mother who had lost her son. She said to me on the day of his funeral,

"I think of what I had, I think of what I lost, and I realize that I have still been very blessed." She explained that he died doing that which he loved, saving human souls. Hemingway wrote, "The world breaks everyone, but some people remain strong in the broken places." The families that I have faced possess a spiritual strength that is without parallel in human life. I may be their rabbi, but in many ways they have taught me the boundless beauty of lasting faith.

One of the most memorable moments in my rabbinical life came when a woman called my office shortly after the World Trade Center tragedy. She was about to give birth and wanted to name her child for one who had lost his life. She then added, "I will try to have more children because I know that there are so many more names." People may not know all the names of the deceased firefighters, but they all know that they owe them their lives.

Someone once explained that goodness and greatness are two independent qualities. Some attain greatness but acquire no goodness. Others amass goodness but never achieve greatness. Firefighters possess both characteristics being great and good.

As a Fire Chaplain, I have tried to bring more tradition into the lives of our firefighters. They, however, have brought more life into the beauty of our tradition. September 11, 2001, has been a defining moment in the history of this country. We have learned to hold on to our memory, hold on to the moment, and, above all, hold on to each other.

MARCIA PRAGER

Congregation P'Nai Or, Philadelphia

Rabbi Prager is a Reconstructionist/ Jewish Renewal teacher, storyteller, and artist living and working in the Mt. Airy community of Philadelphia. She serves as rabbi of the Philadelphia P'Nai Or Renewal Congregation, and is the founding rabbi of a sister congregation, P'Nai Or of Princeton, N.J. She is the director and dean of the ALEPH Rabbinic program. Her newest book is *The Path of Blessing.*

"I am an unconventional rabbi. No one institution or synagogue employs me. I run, what you might call, a one-rabbi outreach program."

I live in Mt. Airy, a thriving Philadelphia neighborhood bursting with Jewish vitality. Here, together with my husband, I raise my family, cook and clean, and–endlessly, it seems–fix up our rambling, old Victorian house.

My home is also, you might say, a mini-yeshiva. Every day, I work with scores of students. Some come for individual study or spiritual direction, many for the semester-length courses I teach throughout the year. I train rabbinical students and community activists; I teach kids and families; I prepare couples for their weddings, plan baby-naming ceremonies, and pray with the ill and bereaved. I rabbi and teach on the margins of Jewish life–to the seekers who have despaired of finding Jewish nourishment and have for so long sought their spiritual fortune only elsewhere, to the un-affiliated, the disappointed, the turned away.

I am an unconventional rabbi. No one institution or synagogue employs me. I run, what you might call, a one-rabbi outreach program. It has generated two vibrant, highly participatory congregations and dozens of study groups. It has embraced passionately dedicated converts and brought talented but marginalized Jews back home into committed Jewish life.

I travel extensively teaching, *davvenen* (praying), and making Shabbos with far-flung communities. I teach Torah, Jewish spiritual practice, and the Jewish God-path to Jews, and also, when I am invited, to Christians. With all my being, I strive not only to teach, but to model a life-embracing, soul-expanding, heart-centered Jewish path that promotes the creative life of the spirit and serves a transformational and healing vision for our whole planet.

When I am not at home, I am traveling around the country and abroad continuing this work. I don't have any grants, and I suppose I am technically "self-employed." But in truth, I am employed and supported by all the amazing people whom I serve.

What is best about my work? I create it! For me, my work really is my art. I constantly hone and shape, learn and grow. The test of its truth comes in the ever-extraordinary moment after a class or a *davvenen*, when I share the tears of sadness and joy that well up in people's eyes as I give over to them a Judaism they never knew, and welcome them home.

The theologian Matthew Fox said that the place God calls you to "is the place where your deep gladness and the world's deep hunger meet." It seems that my deep gladness is to do this work, to go forth and teach, to serve God by co-creating a Jewish spiritual renaissance and a healing for the wounded Jewish soul.

My rabbinate and my work as a Jewish educator is an expression of my soul's desire to perfect our world, to build new models of community, to live a deeply spiritual Jewish life, to serve the Jewish people, and to reach toward God.

SALLY PRIESAND

Monmouth Reform Temple, Tinton Falls, N.J. and America's first woman rabbi

Rabbi Priesand's commitment to all things Jewish, to the cause of justice and peace, to equal opportunity for women, to the needs of the hungry and the homeless, and to the survival of Israel, is reflected in her many organizational affiliations. She is the author of *Judaism and the New Woman* and a contributor to *Women Rabbis: Exploration and Celebration.*

"I have had to face many varied challenges, but I have never regretted my decision to become a rabbi."

I decided I wanted to be a rabbi when I was sixteen years old. Unfortunately, I don't remember why. I do remember always wanting to be a teacher, and my plans always seemed to call for me to teach whatever my favorite subject was at a particular time. One year, I dreamed of being a math teacher, and the next, a teacher of English, or perhaps French. In the end, I decided to be a teacher of Judaism, which is really what a rabbi is.

Fortunately for me, my parents gave me one of the greatest gifts a parent can give a child: the courage to dare and to dream. As a result, I remained focused on my goal, unconcerned that no woman had ever been ordained rabbi by a theological seminary—and determined to succeed despite the doubts I heard expressed in the organized Jewish community. In those days, I did not think very much about being a pioneer, nor was it my intention to champion the rights of women. I just wanted to be a rabbi.

I have had to face many varied challenges, but I have never regretted my decision to become a rabbi. My life has clearly been enriched by the people I have been privileged to serve these past three decades. One of the reasons I enjoy being a congregational rabbi is the opportunity it gives me to read Torah aloud from the *bima* each week and to explore with my congregants the meaning of the text. Whenever I do so, I remember Sinai, that central event in the history of our people, when we made God's law our own.

I also recall a special moment in my life, one that happened just prior to my ordination as a rabbi. The ceremony of ordination was a public event, but it was preceded two days before by a private ceremony held in the chapel of the Hebrew Union College-Jewish Institute of Religion, in Cincinnati. In this private ceremony, each member of my class was handed the Torah scroll by Dr. Alfred Gottschalk, president of the College-Institute. Individually, one by one, we received Torah, and while holding it close to our hearts, affirmed our commitment to the values it represents and to our desire to serve God and the Jewish people. It was a powerful moment for me, in some ways more meaningful than the actual ceremony of ordination. I have never forgotten it, and over the years, whenever I read Torah or take it from the Ark, I feel as if I am receiving it anew.

Having just celebrated the twenty-ninth anniversary of my ordination—and my twentieth year as rabbi of Monmouth Reform Temple in Tinton Falls, New Jersey—I am grateful to God that part of my life's work has been to open new doors for women in the Jewish community. At the same time, I have tried never to lose sight of the larger mission of the Jewish people: to derive from the words of Torah a set of values and a sense of holiness that will enable us always to be partners with God in completing the world.

SHMUEL RABINOWITZ
Rabbi of the Kotel (the Western Wall) and Holy Places, Israel

Rabbi Rabinowitz is the rabbi of the kotel (Western Wall) and other Jewish holy places in Israel such as Masada.

"It is my responsibility as the Rabbi of the Western Wall to protect and preserve its holiness, its religious and spiritual aspects."

Born and bred in Jerusalem, I attended various local yeshivas throughout my formative years, and completed my studies at the renowned Kol Torah Yeshiva in Jerusalem, headed by the distinguished Rabbi Shlomo Zalman Auerbach, of blessed memory. I was ordained as a rabbi by the Chief Rabbinate of Israel and other rabbis of renown. Following my ordination, I was appointed as a regional rabbi for neighborhoods in southwest Jerusalem, a position I retained for three years. My duties there included aiding new immigrants to Israel from the former Soviet Union and Ethiopia.

During this time, I published dozens of articles in various publications about Jewish law, as it pertains to the Western Wall and the holy sites of Israel. Additionally, I have written on many topics of Jewish law itself, such as those pertaining to medicinal issues and the laws of tithing.

Upon the passing of Rabbi Meir Yehudah Getz, of blessed memory, former rabbi of the Western Wall and the Holy Sites of Israel, on the 23rd of Elul, 5755 (Fall, 1995), I was appointed to the position by the chief rabbis of Israel, Rabbi Eliyahu Bakshi Doron and Rabbi Israel Meir Lau. The appointment was also endorsed and supported by the rabbis and Torah Sages of many branches of Judaism in Israel, including the former chief rabbis: Rabbi Avraham Shapira, Rabbi Mordechai Eliyahyu, and Rabbi Ovadiah Yosef; the Kabbalist Rabbi Kaduri; the heads of the Council of Torah Sages of Agudath Israel: Rabbi Elyahsiv, Rabbi Steinman, the Rabbi of Viznitz, and numerous other rabbis.

The Westen Wall serves as a central focal point of prayer for the Jewish people. Untold numbers of Jews—Israelis and tourists—visit the Wall regularly. It has been the holiest site for Jews since the destruction of the Second Temple, the place where G-d's presence never departs. It is my responsibility as the Rabbi of the Western Wall to protect and preserve its holiness, its religious and spiritual aspects.

This accountability includes establishing set prayers for Jews of various branches, such as Ashkenazim, Sephardim, and Hassidim. It includes the logistics of arranging the many public events that are scheduled to take place at the Western Wall, receiving the authorization from the appropriate authorities, assuring safety, and maintaining the proper decorum as befitting the holiness of the site. Additionally, it is my responsibility to ensure that political issues do not detract from the sacredness of the Wall. This is especially relevant today, in light of the fact that the core issue of the Israeli-Arab conflict is the fate and ownership of the area around the Western Wall.

Similar responsibilities apply to many of the holy sites in Israel. My appointment as rabbi of the Holy Sites incorporates dozens of graves of Talmudic-era sages. These include the tombs of Rabbi Shimon bar Yochai in Meron and Rabbi Yonatan ben Uziel in Amuka, both of which are visited by hundreds of thousands of Jews annually.

EMANUEL RACKMAN
Former president and chancellor, Bar Ilan University, Israel

When I was a teen, all my friends were shocked that I spoke of wanting to be a Hebrew teacher. It shocked them that instead of wanting to become a lawyer or doctor or businessman, I had chosen the least popular profession for a Jewish boy. Yet the truth must be told that I had already studied almost the entire Hebrew Bible in the original Hebrew. I was proficient in Hebrew grammar, and I also had a wonderful introduction to the literature of the Talmud, in which my father was an expert.

As a result, after my bar mitzvah, I insisted that I be sent to New York to continue my studies at the Hebrew high schools of Brooklyn or Manhattan. I graduated in 1927 from Talmudic Academy, the preparatory school for Yeshiva University. But instead of going on to YU, I attended Columbia U.– the beginning of a dual career that was to last most of my life. I studied philosophy at Columbia while simultaneously continuing my talmudic studies. In the early '30s, I was ordained as a rabbi.

I married my late wife, Ruth, when she was nineteen and I was twenty. In order to support ourselves, I did, indeed, become a pulpit rabbi in two communities. I continued working toward a Ph.D. and law degree, and assumed I would leave the pulpit to practice law when I was admitted to the bar. But my rabbinical experience was quite pleasant, and when World War II broke out, I could not stand to sit by as so many young men were sent overseas, and so I enlisted as a chaplain.

Still thinking I would someday leave the rabbinate for law, several experiences led me to switch career paths. I found as a chaplain that the condition of Jewish youth in America was sad. In addition, serving in Germany in 1945, I also witnessed the Holocaust; I later worked with Holocaust survivors, and was able to use my legal education to work for postwar reparations and restitution.

When the war ended, Dr. Samuel Belkin, the president of Yeshiva University, asked me to become the rabbi of a wonderful congregation in Far Rockaway, N.Y. I was installed as the rabbi there in 1946 and five years later was given a life contract. Dr. Belkin also invited me to teach government and American law at Yeshiva College.

At the same time, I remained with the military as a chaplain. I was asked to resign my commission in the period of McCarthy. I refused, and insisted on a hearing, in which I claimed I was not a communist but a "civil libertarian." I was allowed to stay and retired in 1960 as a full colonel.

I loved my rabbinic work. I loved preaching. I also loved writing: I published three books on Judaism, and wrote a column for *The Jewish Week*– over 1,000 articles–that many readers told me had a deep impact on them. Above all, I was able to help large numbers of young people find their ways as Jews and as Orthodox Jews. I was determined not only to raise an Orthodox Jewish family, but to help students to cherish their heritage and come closer to Jewish living and Jewish thought.

When I was already planning to retire, I was offered the presidency of Bar Ilan University, a university that offers both religious and secular education–another example of the dual path to which I was dedicated. So we moved to Israel in 1977, and lived there for more than twenty years.

Throughout my career, I was an outspoken exponent of Modern Orthodoxy–the idea that traditional, orthodox Judaism can exist comfortably alongside modern, secular society. Some historians have even deemed me the founder of Modern Orthodoxy. While I was at YU, however, the president tried to convince me to call it "centrist" rather than "modern," but I resisted: Some of my views were downright extremist, not centrist, for an Orthodox person, especially since I was an outspoken feminist.

One of the biggest controversies between me and the Orthodox establishment came over the issue of divorce in Jewish law. According to traditional law, only the husband can grant a divorce, leading some men to withhold divorce documents out of vindictiveness, or as blackmail for money or custody of their children. I broke with the majority of Orthodox rabbis and established a rabbinical court that would annul such marriages. Despite my advocacy of Modern Orthodoxy, however, I have always opposed the factionalism and denominationalism of Judaism. I have, and always will, support every effort for Jewish unity.

URI REGEV

Executive Director, World Union for Progressive Judaism

Rabbi Regev is the Executive Director of the World Union for Progressive Judaism and is the former head of the Israel Religious Action Center.

"I am increasingly aware of the new and continuing challenges here and around the world, particularly in Eastern Europe and the former Soviet Union, in places which have been cut-off for decades from mainstream Jewish life."

A s this book goes to print, I am taking on a new responsibility. After leading the Israel Religious Action Center (IRAC), the Reform movement's advocacy arm in Israel, I am now directing the World Union for Progressive Judaism, the umbrella organization of the Reform, Liberal, Progressive, and Reconstructionist movements around the world.

While I was still director of IRAC, *Yated Ne'eman*–an ultra-Orthodox newspaper–published an unsolicited, somewhat distorted "testimonial" to my work. In a five-page "exposé" in September 1999 entitled "The Reform Movement's invasion of Eretz Yisroel (the Land of Israel)," the paper wrote:

"The Torah community's relatively complacent response to the Reform Movement's current offensive is an indicator that many of us remain unaware to the deep inroads that our spiritual enemies have made in recent years. Well, the time has come to snap out of our fantasy. If we wait any longer, Eretz Yisroel may soon change beyond recognition. Who are the invaders, and how are they attempting to undermine the authority of Torah-true Judaism in Eretz Yisroel? The Reform Movement's current all-out offensive is being choreographed, directed and funded by the Assoc. of Reform Zionists of America (ARZA), and its Israeli subsidiary IRAC, which is headed by Uri Regev."

Our ongoing commitment is to the founding principle of Israel–as stated in its Declaration of Independence–as the Jewish State "based on the precepts of liberty, justice and peace as taught by the Hebrew Prophets," a land that ensures "complete social and political equality to all its inhabitants irrespective of religion, race, or gender," and which guarantees "freedom of religion and conscience." These ideals are precisely what are being attacked by *Yated Ne'eman* as "undermining the authority of Torah-true Judaism in Eretz Yisroel."

The vision of freedom of religious conscience stands in stark contrast to the painful reality where Israel is the only democracy that still denies Jews full religious freedom. Because of the politically tangled status quo, Israeli law entrusts all authority in matters of marriage to the Orthodox rabbinate. Hundreds of thousands of Israeli citizens are denied their civil and human right to marry, though most Israelis consistently and clearly express their preference for freedom of choice and religious pluralism.

I, like most Israelis who were raised in a secular environment, realized that Judaism's worst enemy in Israel is religious coercion and politicization, which is imposed by a strident minority. I was sixteen years old when I first discovered, as an exchange student to the U.S., that Judaism is a pluralistic, dynamic, rich, evolving tradition, rather than an all-or-nothing creed.

I have dedicated many years to expanding religious pluralism in Israel, and the *Yated Ne'eman* attack is only one indication that much progress has been made. While there are many spurious attacks in the press, there are many more expressions of support from all segments of Israeli society. Many, even in the Orthodox community, understand that the unholy alliance between religion and state damages both state and religion.

The onslaught, though, is accelerating as polls show that a clear majority of Israelis support religious diversity, non-Orthodox weddings and conversions, and generally support granting equal status to Reform and Conservative Judaism with that of that of Orthodoxy.

When we founded IRAC, we chose as its subtitle: "For Human Equality, Social Justice and Religious Tolerance." Our unwritten motto has been, "We don't take no for an answer." I am taking these guiding principles with me to my new position.

I am increasingly aware of the new and continuing challenges here and around the world, particularly in Eastern Europe and the former Soviet Union, in places which have been cut-off for decades from mainstream Jewish life.

There is critical need, especially outside North America, to present to the world and to the Jewish community, in the face of growing assimilation, a progressive religious alternative reconciling the ancient tradition, modernity, and democracy rooted in a commitment to social justice. I will work to meet this need in the spirit of cooperation, tolerance, and respect for those within and outside the Jewish community, yet never shying away from doing "what is just and right."

MARTIN ROZENBERG

Rabbi Emeritus, The Community Synagogue, Port Washington, N.Y.

Rabbi Rozenberg is a member of the Bible translation committee of the Jewish Publication Society that produced the New Jewish Version and is the author of *Psalms: A New Translation and Commentary.* He is the former National Chairman of the Commission on Jewish Education, The Union of American Hebrew Congregations.

"When he saw the puzzled look upon my face, he bent over and whispered in my ear the Yiddish word 'massernik,' meaning informer. It was unsettling to actually see a fellow Jew in this traitorous role."

There are certain moments in the life of a rabbi that define for him the importance and responsibility of his role. For me, meeting the Jews of Tashkent was such a moment. Tashkent, at the time of our visit, was part of the former Soviet Union. During World War II, the Soviets transplanted Jews from the region around the city of Minsk and sent them to Tashkent. There, they lived isolated under rigid Soviet control. Most American Jews who traveled to the Soviet Union limited their visits to European Russia, which normally included Moscow and Leningrad. Few Jewish visitors ventured into Asian Russia, but that is where I went.

I was accompanied by a group from my congregation, the Community Synagogue of Port Washington, N.Y. For these Jews of Tashkent, feeling so utterly truncated from the rest of the world Jewish community, our visit was a ray of light in an otherwise bleak existence. Although these Russian Jews spoke only Yiddish, and with the exception of myself, no one in our group spoke Yiddish, an immediate Jewish bonding took place between us. We all knew that we were part of the same *mishpacha* (family) and felt we were visiting with relatives. They were eager to hear us speak about how vibrant and dynamic Jewish life in America. It was clear that as they were listening they were contrasting in their heads the rosy picture I painted with their own sad lot. I therefore assured them that there were seismic changes taking place in the rest of the world, and that their isolation and exile would soon come to an end. Some, with tears in their eyes, responded, "Amen." I was deeply moved that as a rabbi, I represented to these Jews a ray of hope, that even if only for a moment, I was able to give them faith and ease their sense of isolation.

We also visited Moscow, and it was an equally moving experience. It was the time of the "refuseniks"–those courageous Russian Jews who proudly asserted their Jewish identity and dared to defy the Communist regime. We met with some refuseniks covertly; all of us became aware in Moscow, as we could not at home, of the heavy psychological oppression under which Russian Jews were forced to live. Our group looked forward to the visit to the synagogue, for we felt that within its walls the Jews we would meet there would be less guarded and willing to express themselves more freely. We were to learn otherwise.

Upon entering the synagogue my eyes were drawn to a small group of men seated at a table studying the Talmud. I took a seat and joined them. They were studying "Sanhedrin," a section of the Talmud with which I was familiar. The man leading the study was not a rabbi but simply a learned Jew. He soon interrupted the studying to inquire about myself and our group. In turn, I began to inquire about Jewish life and living conditions for them as Jews, feeling that it was safe to do so in the intimate synagogue setting in which we found ourselves. I was rather taken aback when the leader placed his finger to his lips signaling silence, and with a motion of his head pointed in the direction of a man leaning silently against the wall. When he saw the puzzled look upon my face, he bent over and whispered in my ear the Yiddish word "massernik," meaning informer. It was unsettling to actually see a fellow Jew in this traitorous role.

I remember well my mixed feelings upon leaving the synagogue. The scene of a small enclave of half a dozen Jews studying Torah under the scrutinizing eyes of a KGB informer was a paradigm for courageous defiance and hope. The Communists sought to extirpate all religion, Judaism included. But these men in the Moscow synagogue were echoing the answer of Jews throughout history who found themselves in similar circumstances, namely, that by nurturing themselves on Torah and holding on to it, they would overcome their enemies and survive. However, I also could not escape a feeling of sadness that overcame me at the realization that what I was beholding was not a dynamic yeshivah with young eager students but rather the flickering flame of a dying candle. At the time no one in our group could have

foreseen that within a few short years it would be Communism that would die and the little flame we beheld would rekindle Jewish life in Russia and Judaism would experience a renaissance among Russian Jews.

As rabbis, the most important "work" we do is not necessarily the functions we perform in the synagogue. Opportunities to serve, teach, heal, and inspire sometimes present themselves in the most unexpected places and circumstances.

The watchful eye of the Soviet secret service agent in this Moscow synagogue is not at all secret. It was a visible presence for Russian Jews and made for a constant awareness of Communist religious oppression that sought to suppress Judaism and Jewish life under Soviet rule. In former historical periods of Jewish persecution, no matter what abuse the Jews suffered on the outside, he could at least find sanctuary in his synagogue where he could openly commune with his God. This spiritual solace was denied the Russian Jews. Even in their synagogues Russian Jews prayed with fear and had to look over their shoulders and speak in whispers. This mental and spiritual enslavement borne by Russian Jews was as heavy a burden as their lack of political freedom.

PETER RUBINSTEIN

Senior Rabbi, Central Synagogue, New York City

Rabbi Rubinstein is the Senior Rabbi at Central Synagogue in New York City, a Reform congregation affiliated with the Union of American Hebrew Congregations. In addition to his professional affiliations and responsibilities, he presently serves as the Rabbinic Co-Chair of the National Commission of Rabbinic-Congregational Relations and on the Alumni Nominating Committee of Amherst College.

"I love my work. As I reported to my congregation at a recent annual meeting, 'I am grateful to God who stays with me every day of my life, and whom I thank constantly for having made me a Jew and led me to the Rabbinate.'"

U pon graduating from Amherst College in 1964, I was determined to pursue a medical and research career. Formed in many ways by my years at the Bronx High School of Science, life to me was clearly determined by the relationship between cause and effect. Once you knew the cause, the outcome would become evident. And if you couldn't find the solution, it meant that you hadn't looked hard enough or spent enough time in search.

Thus my attraction to research, the lovely "simplicity" of it all–and I wouldn't have to deal with people, which was an asset for an inherently shy twenty year old.

Well, somewhere along the way I got lost. In fact, what happened was a conversation with Dr. Eugene Borowitz, to whom I had been referred by my older brother, who was in rabbinic school at the time of my college graduation. My brother fretted that I had written my senior thesis about the systematic theologian Paul Tillich and that I had come under the influence of a fabulous college professor in the religion department with whom I had studied everything about modern Christian thought. In response to my question of my brother–"So, what do Jews believe?"– he sputtered a bit before sending me on to Dr. Borowitz.

I met Dr. Borowitz, a foremost Jewish theologian, in a bar on the West Side of Manhattan. Having steeled myself with a mug of beer, I asked, my question, "What do Jews believe?"

"If you want to learn that," Dr. Borowitz said with a look that hovered between disbelief and humor, "you need to come to the Hebrew Union College-Jewish Institute of Religion."

I applied and was accepted into HUC-JIR and postponed my entry into a joint M.D./Ph.D. program. That's the story.

Actually, my studies moved seamlessly from a concentration on theology to a fascination with history. For that I am indebted to Dr. Martin Cohen, also a professor at HUC-JIR. I found my studies with him a way to integrate the "causal" relationship with an understanding of Jewish thought. But even after pursuing doctoral studies, I decided that my life needed to live among Jews, in the "trenches" of Jewish life, the synagogue.

For the most part I have divided my rabbinate into decade segments, having spent the '70s in a fabulous congregation in Westchester County outside of New York City, the '80s in a terrific congregation in San Mateo, California, outside of San Francisco, and the last decade and more at Central Synagogue, where I have settled. I love my work. As I reported to my congregation at a recent annual meeting, "I am grateful to God who stays with me every day of my life, and whom I thank constantly for having made me a Jew and led me to the Rabbinate. My professional life is my way of thanking our ancestors for having brought us this far."

The life of a rabbi is replete with unexpected joys and challenges. Sadly, the sanctuary of Central Synagogue was ravished by fire in 1998, leading to the need for a complete restoration and dedication on September 9, 2001, just two days prior to the tragedies of September 11. The fire was a trauma. The murders at the World Trade Center are a tragedy. Yet the response to both needed to include vision, hope, and an enthusiastic embrace of life and our faith. The rebuilding of our sanctuary called on skills I never needed prior to the fire. The project taught me much about the essential connections between architecture and prayer, and mandated that our congregation think deliberately and creatively about the place of the spiritual and sacred in our personal and collective life.

But the rebuilding of our sanctuary also became a symbol. Everything but life can be rebuilt. And while nothing is equivalent to a tragic loss of life, we need to be firm in our resolve to always rebuild our lives continuously and to meticulously weave the stories and memories of those who have died before us into the fabric of our own being.

DAVID SAPERSTEIN
Director of the Religious Action Center of Reform Judaism

The head of the Reform movement's Religious Action Center, Rabbi Saperstein is a leading activist and voice of spirit and conscience in public affairs. He has dedicated his life and career to fighting for public policies that reflect Reform Judaism's liberal social conscience. He resides in Washington, D.C.

"I feel daily blessed that I have been able to spend my career helping to bring the voice of justice from a committed and caring Jewish community into the deliberations of those decisions to shape the priorities and direction of this nation."

Three thousand years ago, the Jewish people brought forth from Sinai a vision that has transformed all of human history. At its core is an ethical monotheism that maintains that we are partners with God in creating a fairer, more just, more compassionate world for all God's children.

As with every generation before us, rabbis today are charged to carry those values into the world–to preach them, to teach them, to live them. That task remains as urgent as it has ever been, perhaps even more than elsewhere here in the most influential and most powerful nation on earth, at a moment in history when fundamental decisions are being shaped about issues as vital and diverse as economic justice, sustainable development, international human rights, the well-being of Israel, and the application of ethics to startling new scientific and technological developments that will change the world.

Those of us who carry the title "rabbi" here in America at the dawn of a new century are both burdened and blessed: We do our sacred work in a land that that has given Jews more freedoms and rights–and hence also more responsibilities–than we have experienced anywhere else in the course of our wanderings, in a land that has become for so many of us a home. And here, as well, we have been invited to discharge our own rendezvous with human history–to speak truth to power, to seek to be a light to the nations.

I feel daily blessed that I have been able to spend my career helping to bring the voice of justice by a committed and caring Jewish community into the deliberations of those decisions to shaping the priorities and direction of this nation.

SOLOMON SCHIFF

Director, Community Chaplaincy Service of the Greater Miami Jewish Federation; Executive Vice President, Rabbinical Association of greater Miami

Rabbi Schiff was ordained by Rabbi Moshe Feinstein of the Mesifta Tefereth Jerusalem Rabbinical Seminary in New York and is a member of the Rabbinical Council of America. He has made numerous TV appearances, and is a regular panelist on Viewpoint, which brings clergy of different faiths together. He is married and has three sons and seven grandchildren.

"I told him I would be glad to, except that the game was to be on Rosh Hashanah. He called me back the next day and told me he got permission to change it to the next night. I told him, embarrassingly, that Rosh Hashanah is a two-day holiday."

I have enjoyed a long and fine association with the Miami Dolphins football team and its founding owner, Joe Robbie. It started when our son, Elliot, won two complimentary tickets to one season's opening game. Since the game was on a Friday night, we sold the tickets. Some time later, Joe and Elizabeth Robbie were guests for dinner in our home, and I interviewed Joe several times on television programs sponsored by the Rabbinical Association of Greater Miami. I have delivered an annual invocation at a Miami Dolphins football game for over twenty-five years.

In the first week in September 1972, after the massacre of eleven Israeli athletes at the Olympics in Munich, Germany, we had a special meeting at the Greater Miami Jewish Federation to discuss mobilizing public opinion against the terrorists. At the meeting, someone suggested that the invocation at the upcoming Dolphins game–which was to be broadcast on national television–be dedicated to the subject of terrorism, as a means of getting the attention of a national audience.

Since I had a close relationship with Joe Robbie, I was asked to call him on this. He told me: "I was in Munich for the games. When this tragedy occurred, I was devastated. All the way home, I kept feeling so frustrated that there is nothing I can do. And here you call me with a suggestion that I can do something. I would like you to do the invocation."

I told him I would be glad to, except that the game was to be on Rosh Hashanah. He called me back the next day and told me he got permission to change it to the next night. I told him, embarrassingly, that Rosh Hashanah is a two-day holiday. "When can we play?" he asked. I said Sunday night, after sundown. He called me back and told me that the best he could do was Sunday at 6 p.m., because of the CBS television schedule. I thanked him for all his efforts, but could not do the invocation anyway. Instead, he told me, the Rev. Edward Graham, a prominent black minister, would offer it. (The prayer was extremely well received. He asked for a moment of silence and then devoted his invocation to the subject. Our federation received numerous calls from around the country lauding us for this coup.)

After this conversation was completed, Mr. Robbie invited me to travel with him and the Dolphins team to New York to attend a game against the New York Jets. I said I would be delighted and would like to take my sons, Elliot and Jeffrey. He agreed, but we ran into the same problem: Since the game was to be on a Sunday, the team would travel on Saturday. We did, however, get to travel back to Florida with the team. It was a very fine experience. It was also historic, since that year was the first "perfect season," in which the Dolphins were 17-0, and won the Super Bowl.

The following year, 1973, Joe Robbie invited my sons and me to travel on his plane with the team to Dallas, when the Dolphins were to play the Dallas Cowboys on Thanksgiving Day. It was a marvelous experience. The Dolphins won and went on to win the Super Bowl in a second consecutive year. In 1983, the Dolphins again went to the Super Bowl, and he invited me to join him on his plane to the big game. On the return flight, he introduced me to his friends, saying, "The rabbi always brings us good luck. What's your record with us?" I said "12-1." His friends were impressed. Joe jokingly asked me, "What happened to the one game you lost?" I said, "I'll tell you, Joe, the way the Dolphins played that day, God himself couldn't help them."

To which he replied, "I'll tell you, Rabbi, if the Dolphins would have prepared their defense as well as yours, they would have won."

JUDITH SCHINDLER

Associate Rabbi, Temple Beth El, Charlotte, N.C.

W henever my father would call me at work, he would love to ask for me by saying, "This is Rabbi Schindler, may I please speak with Rabbi Schindler?" While I was at times embarrassed by his fatherly pride in my choice of career, that feeling was far overshadowed by my infinite respect for who he was and what he stood for. For he was not only my father, he was a great rabbi–a leader in the Jewish world. And he was not only my father, he was my teacher.

Just as my father taught me, so did his father teach him. My grandfather, Eliezer Schindler, was a social activist, who in the early 1930s in Nazi Germany was unafraid to speak out publicly against Hitler and his regime. As a poet, my grandfather taught my father the beauty of song and the written word. As an activist, he taught my father to speak out against injustice, no matter what the cost. As a thinker, he taught my father how to see beyond what is–how to be a visionary. And as an *Ohev Yisrael*–lover of Israel–he taught his son how to love the Jewish people with abounding love.

My father learned and lived these lessons well. In his role as a leader of the Reform movement for more than twenty years, he made it his mission to draw people into the fold of Jewish life rather than writing them out. He took upon himself the charge of welcoming into Judaism many of those who had traditionally been cast out. He made a home in Judaism for those who are of patrilineal descent–people born to a Jewish father but not a Jewish mother, traditionally considered not Jewish. Likewise, he made a home in our synagogues for those who were in interfaith marriages, and he made room in our pulpits for women and gay clergy.

Ironically, I was just a child during those years when women were first ordained and my father was fighting for their rights. Becoming a rabbi had never crossed my mind because I had never met a woman rabbi. It was not until years later that I came to know several successful female rabbis and realized that the rabbinate could be a path in which I, too, could follow.

My father was best known for his warm embrace–not only to his nine grandchildren, five children, and beloved wife, Rhea, but to his friends, colleagues, acquaintances, and even to those who stood at a distance. He was there for Jews throughout the world who were in distress. He consistently responded with action to Jonathan Pollard's weekly, if not, at times, daily phone calls for support–to help release him from what my father considered an unjust sentence. (Pollard was convicted of spying on the U.S. for Israel and sentenced to life in prison.)

In Judaism, merit is given to the one who attributes their sources. In studying the Talmud, one can get exhausted from the long list of attributions. A typical phrase might read: "Raba said in the name of Rav Sehorah who said in the name of Rav Huna." I've always wondered why the sages took such pains to mention the scholarly chain that transmitted their knowledge. But now as I teach on my own, I find myself constantly wanting to tell everyone from whom most of my teachings come, for they come from my father. He taught me how to preach, how to teach, how to be a rabbi, spouse, parent, and *mensch*. Not a day goes by when I do not read a text upon which he expounded. In the Talmud it states that "every scholar who is quoted in this world, his lips whisper from the grave." My father continues to speak to me as I share the teachings that he once taught.

There is a Yiddish folk saying that tells us that death does not take the time to knock on the door, sometimes our loved ones are stolen from us. My father was stolen from this world and far too soon. He left this world peacefully in November of 2000 at the age of seventy-five. He wrote that, "Whenever one gate of life closes, God makes sure to open another. No purpose is served in rattling closed gates and bemoaning the past. Far better to walk through those newly opened gates."

With his death, tears were shed worldwide. For through his life he had brought smiles and warmth to so many–enabling those from afar to find their home in Judaism and those who were close to find their home in his heart.

Zecher tzadik l'vrachah–may the memory of the righteous be a blessing.

ARTHUR SCHNEIER

Senior Rabbi, Park East Synagogue, New York City; President,
Appeal of Conscience Foundation

Internationally known for his leadership on behalf of religious freedom and human rights, Rabbi Schneier has worked for religious freedom and tolerance throughout the world.

"For the last forty years, I have shared the joys and sorrows of my people from the cradle to the grave."

A s a rabbi, I have always seen my greatest challenge–and my greatest responsibility– as working to ensure Jewish continuity and survival. The Park East Synagogue, where I have been the rabbi since 1962, is a historic landmark congregation that was founded in 1890. But despite its illustrious past, it had few children, and therefore, I feared, little hope for the future. To attract more youth, we acquired the property adjacent to the synagogue and established the Arthur Schneier Park East Day School. The school's theme song is "L'dor Vador"–from generation to generation. Indeed, the children have not only learned the Torah values of their ancestors, but many have also brought their parents back to Judaism and strengthened their whole family's Jewish identity.

In 1964, at the height of the communist oppression in the Soviet Union, I was pained by the government's attempts to bring about the extinction of Soviet Jewry. They closed synagogues and prohibited Jewish education. Remembering the Talmudic dictum, "one Jew is responsible for another," I rallied Christian and Jewish leaders and public officials in an "Appeal of Conscience" on behalf of Soviet Jewry; we bought a full-page *New York Times* ad and organized the first demonstration on behalf of Soviet Jewry, which took place in front of our synagogue, opposite our new neighbor–the Soviet mission to the U.N. Declaring, "Let my people go, and let my people live," I was joined by Senator Robert Kennedy and Mayor Robert Wagner in affixing a plaque to our synagogue, reading: "Hear the cry of the oppressed, the Jewish community in the Soviet Union."

Soon after, I founded the Appeal of Conscience Foundation, an interfaith coalition of business and religious leaders committed to religious freedom and human rights. One of the greatest moments was obtaining permission for ten rabbinic students from the Soviet Union to study in Budapest at the only rabbinic seminary in Eastern Europe. Its first graduate, Rabbi Adolf Shayevich, became Chief Rabbi of Russia.

A highlight of my struggle for religious freedom was the restoration of the Shanghai Ohel Rachel Synagogue in 1998. Visiting Shanghai as part of President Clinton's delegation to China, I visited the newly restored synagogue with First Lady Hillary Rodham Clinton and Secretary of State Madeline Albright. While there, I placed in the ark a Torah Scroll donated by the Park East Synagogue to the Jewish community of Shanghai. For the first time since World War II, Rosh Hashanah services were held at Ohel Rachel synagogue.

For the last forty years, I have shared the joys and sorrows of my people from the cradle to the grave. The joys of birth, growth into adulthood, and marriage give everyone pleasure, and I am thrilled to be part of this aspect of my congregants' lives. But as a rabbi, I must also bring hope and comfort to those living through the tragic events that we sometimes experience in life. The horrific terrorist attack on the World Trade Center on September 11, with its unprecedented devastation, forced me to expand my role far beyond my congregational family and to give comfort and healing to all New Yorkers. To do this, I drew upon my experience as a Holocaust survivor and worked to help people understand that no matter how terrifying an experience is, you pick up the pieces of shattered lives and move on.

At Yankee Stadium, where the playing field was transformed into a praying field, I addressed thousands of mourning families who lost loved ones. It became my sad mission to visit Ground Zero to encourage the firefighters, police officers, and other rescue workers as they toiled around the clock. At the reopening of the Mercantile Exchange, standing side by side with Gov. George Pataki and Mayor Giuliani, I encouraged the members of the exchange by saying, "Our hearts may be broken, but our spirit will enable us to rebuild. We will emerge from tragedy even stronger, with faith and hope in the future."

With unshakable faith throughout my life, I have turned heavenward to God, my guardian and anchor. However, one's life mission cannot be limited to the Divine. We have a responsibility to one another; together all God's children have the challenge of helping Him perfect an imperfect world.

MARC SCHNEIER

President, Foundation for Ethnic Understanding; founding rabbi,
The Hampton Synagogue, Westhampton Beach, N.Y.

Instrumental in healing the rift between blacks and Jews, Rabbi Schneier met secretly with Louis Farrakhan recently in an effort to reconcile Jews with the Nation of Islam. As a rabbi in the Hamptons, he is also something of a "rabbi to the stars," leading the services attended by the likes of Steven Spielberg attend when he is in the Hamptons.

"The common thread that runs through my activities is the need for people of all denominations, persuasions, ethnicities, and religions to recognize the strength that comes from sharing our similarities and differences."

I am the eighteenth generation of rabbis in my family. I fulfilled a childhood dream and was ordained at Yeshiva University. I have a great passion for Judaism, for the need to channel one's energy, talents, and resources in Jewish leadership.

I have always championed the cause of Jewish unity. There are so many issues that transcend our religious, theological, and ideological differences. I advocated these principles when I served as president of the New York Board of Rabbis and in my current tenure as president of the North American Boards of Rabbis. There are two areas in which a rabbi should look to contribute: the spiritual realm and the political realm. In the spiritual realm, I believe I have made a contribution by building The Hampton Synagogue and transforming Jewish life in the Hamptons. In the political realm, I chose to focus on the new reality of changing demographics in the United States and the need for the Jewish community to strengthen its relationships with other ethnicities.

I define my rabbinate as the rabbi of an Orthodox synagogue with a Conservative congregation and a Reform membership. That encapsulates the very eclectic nature of The Hampton Synagogue. The synagogue began when I was vacationing in the Hamptons in 1990 and rented a summer home. I had some people join me for services in the living room. The village tried to shut us down alleging violations of zoning and fire laws, so we persevered, formally organized as a synagogue and dedicated a building in 1994. Today, in season, 600 people attend services every Saturday morning. Many local celebrities have been supportive of our efforts, including Steven Spielberg, Marvin Hamlisch, and Wendy Wasserstein.

I have witnessed a transformation in my rabbinate. In the founding years of the synagogue, I focused on sensitizing the non-Orthodox community of the Hamptons to Orthodoxy. Today, it has evolved to re-educating the Orthodox, many of whom have bought homes there, to embrace the principles inclusiveness and tolerance.

I believe one of the great challenges facing the American Jewish community is the changing demographics of the United States. For example, New York City is only thirty-eight percent white; demographers are forecasting that the minority communities of today–African-Americans and Latinos–will constitute a majority of the country within fifty years. This is a significant development in terms of the Jewish community's alliances. We need to rebuild the historic black-Jewish partnership, and with the Latino community, we must build new bridges. In these two areas, the Foundation for Ethnic Understanding is in the vanguard. In 1989, I established the Foundation for Ethnic Understanding with the late Broadway producer and impresario Joseph Papp. Twelve years later, the foundation is nationally recognized for its leadership and efforts in strengthening relations between the Jewish community and other ethnic groups. As chairman of the World Jewish Congress Commission on Intergroup Relations, I have been able to disseminate these efforts on a global level.

The common thread that runs through my activities is the need for people of all denominations, persuasions, ethnicities, and religions to recognize the strength that comes from sharing our similarities and differences. No one should ever possess the arrogance to believe that his or her way is the only way. We can and must learn from others. This has been the hallmark and the teaching of my rabbinate.

ORI YEHUDAH YOSEPH SCHONTHAL

Director, Beth Rivkah Girls Seminary, Yerres, France

Rabbi Schonthal is the Director of the Beth Rivkah Girls Seminary, in Yerres, France, which trains special education teachers.

"Today, some of those children are now grandparents, some are successful businessmen, while others are rabbis and other professionals. We meet them from time to time in the most unexpected places, and they remind us of the 'good old times.'"

When my wife and I had been married about two years, I quit a teaching job in Westchester County, New York, and we moved to Paris. Here we both ran a Talmud Torah (Hebrew School–Youth Center combination) in the picturesque Montmartre area, not far from a public square where French "artists" would make a fast buck by drawing sketches and caricatures of American tourists.

This was back in the early 1960s. At the time, Jews were fleeing their long-established homes in Morocco and Algeria because of the crisis in Israel, which affected their previously good relationship with the Arabs. Many of these refugees moved into tiny apartments in our area. There was a great shortage of jobs and money, and the fact that we busied ourselves taking care of their children was like an injection of oxygen for them.

Today, some of those children are now grandparents, some are successful businessmen, while others are rabbis and other professionals. We meet them from time to time in the most unexpected places, and they remind us of the "good old times."

We lived on the premises of our center, which was called "Le Merkaz de Montmartre," and we raised three of our children there. We also had on the premises a small–but heavily attended–synagogue.

One evening, at about 11 p.m., there was an insistent ringing and knocking at the main door, downstairs. I went to see who it was, and there I found a young Jewish couple, both very agitated. "We have come so that my wife can swear in front of the Torah scroll," declared the husband. I found this a strange request, especially at that late hour, but I invited them into our little flat, where my wife served them hot drinks. I insisted that before I lead them into the synagogue, they explain their behavior. After much prodding, I found out that the husband was very jealous because his wife's boss had invited her to lunch in a restaurant, and she had accepted. My wife took the woman aside and talked to her privately, and I did the same with the man. After about two hours, they both calmed down, and left us looking much happier than when they had come.

This was but one small incident among the many from over the years. Some have been funny, some sad, and some tragic. But this one incident sticks out in my mind, because it stimulated us into spending nearly forty years–so far–offering marriage counseling to the people who look to us for rabbinic guidance.

ISMAR SCHORSCH
Chancellor, Jewish Theological Seminary of America, New York City

Rabbi Schorsch is the sixth Chancellor of the Jewish Theological Seminary and its Rabbi Herman Abramovitz Professor of Jewish History. The chancellor of the Jewish Theological Seminary is the titular head of Conservative Judaism, and Rabbi Schorsch has used the position to take an active role in public affairs and political advocacy.

"The role model of my father attuned me to the presence of God in the forms of Judaism. Revelation builds upon a predisposition."

According to the Midrash, God addressed Moses at the burning bush in the voice of his father in order not to frighten him in this first encounter. The comment, though, points to a deeper truth, that it is our parents who determine the eventual nature of our relationship to God. I love to study, but my faith did not spring from books. I chose to become a rabbi because I really had no choice. The role model of my father attuned me to the presence of God in the forms of Judaism. Revelation builds upon a predisposition.

My father embodied the best of the German rabbinate. His Judaism pulsated with prayer and praxis, study and good deeds, deep Jewish learning and broad general knowledge. The carnage of World War I, which he witnessed briefly as an adolescent in the German army on the western front in 1918, drove him to embrace a life of faith. Only religion, he felt, could stay the impulse to self-destruct. Judaism became the ballast of his life.

After earning a doctorate from Tübingen and ordination from the Breslau Seminary, he assumed the post of associate rabbi in Hanover. The absence of an organ in its magnificent Romanesque synagogue was to his liking. For nearly a decade he focused much of his effort on reconnecting alienated young Jews with the synagogue. In the organizational settings he helped them create and administer, he insisted on full equality between German Jews and Eastern European immigrants, of which there were many in Hanover. In the Gemeinde the latter gained membership only after the Nazis came to power. My father had grown up amid the unpretentious piety of village Jews in Baden and felt an affinity for the davening of the Ostjuden in their *stieblach*. Testimony to his impact are the many Hanoverians I have met over the years who related to me what my father meant to them in their youth.

In the summer of 1933, the Gemeinde sent my father to Palestine to determine how best to prepare the young for aliyah. After his death, I discovered the pocket diary in which he prosaically and sparingly took note of sights seen and conservations had. No trace of any intention to return. How utterly different would my life have been if in those fateful years my family had decided to go east instead of west. But my father was an unpolitical man, determined not to abandon his besieged flock.

A visa to England rescued my father from Buchenwald after Kristallnacht. That year we lit the first light of Hanukkah in Germany and the second in England. Prohibited from working, my father set about to learn English. By the time we arrived in the States in March 1940, he was ready to take a pulpit. A small Conservative congregation of Jews from Eastern Europe in Pottstown, Pennsylvania, invited him and he stayed until his retirement twenty-four years later.

The playing field had shrunk but not his devotion to the rabbinate. He quickly mastered the multiple tasks of being a full-service rabbi. He ran a five-day-a-week Hebrew school and delivered two sermons every Shabbat. Singlehandedly, he published the congregational bulletin. He attended the daily minyan morning and evening, visited the sick, officiated at weddings and funerals, comforted the bereaved and counseled the troubled. He even found time to train a choir and to speak for Judaism to the Christian community. For many years he also served as the Jewish chaplain at the Valley Forge Army Hospital, deriving lasting satisfaction from aiding the human wreckage of war in its painful and often prolonged recovery.

Like Judaism itself, the religion of my father consisted of polarities in balance. His meticulous observance of the norms of Judaism was informed by a philosopher's conception of God. Maimonides, Spinoza, and Kant were his constant companions. So was the Bible, which he studied daily and revered as a kaleidoscope of religious experience. But the language of God was not restricted to Jewish sacred texts. He felt its power in the grandeur of science and the beauty of nature. In short, he lived like a pietist but studied like a humanist. Though he died twenty years ago, we often meet in the pages of his books that are scattered throughout my library.

SHLOMO SCHWARTZ
Founder and Director, Chai Center, Los Angeles

Rabbi Schwartz was born in Atlantic City, New Jersey. His father was the cantor of the Chelsea Hebrew Congregation, a conservative temple. Rabbi Schwartz became a follower of the Rebbe and was a campus rabbi at UCLA for nineteen years. He now specializes in outreach to non-affiliates. He is married and has twelve children.

"I still do not know why their beloved son died, or why this led to their return to their Jewish roots. But it was not the first time I have seen death and tragedy lead people to Judaism."

A s a rabbi, I do a lot of lifecycle events, known affectionately in the trade as "hatch 'em, match 'em, and dispatch 'em." I specialize in Jews not affiliated with Jewish organizations or denominations, which includes about seventy percent of Los Angeles' Jews. The most difficult of these, of course, are the tragedies. When the situation involves the death of a child, the inexplicability of the tragedy leaves the religious leader, to whom the family turns, at a loss for words.

On a seemingly uneventful day, I got a call from a friend who is a brilliant therapist and Torah scholar. She had never called me for help, and when she did, I knew it would be challenging. A young couple was walking on the beach near their home in Malibu when their eight-year-old suddenly collapsed and died. Their therapist and friend asked me to accompany her to their home to help. This was not a mission for which I had any enthusiasm, since I had no answers to offer them. Besides, they had almost no Jewish background with which I could begin any sort of dialogue involving traditional wisdom and theology.

When I walked into their lovely beach home, I expected them to direct their anger and hostility at me as the target for their intense emotions. But I thought that if I could even just play this role for them, it would be a service to grieving parents. They had never met a rabbi and were devoid of religion, and they received me with curiosity and respect. I remember thinking, "I have virtually nothing to offer this family; what do I say now?" In my heart, I offered a silent prayer: "Dearest all-powerful One, give me the words or get me out of here!" Somehow, though, I must have helped them. This encounter began a deep, personal relationship that further developed when they sought to have a *bris* for their subsequent newborn son. The husband later retired from his job in the construction industry to begin a new career—as a rabbi.

Thinking back on the painful moments of my first meeting with this family, when I walked into their house of tragic death, I had no explanation, no rationalization, to offer them. I still do not know why their beloved son died, or why this led to their return to their Jewish roots. But it was not the first time I have seen death and tragedy lead people to Judaism.

In 1980, I was in charge of a Jewish homeless program, doing the initial interviews to see if the would-be clients were eligible for ninety days of shelter. In this capacity, I met Charlie Foner, an absolutely charming and good-looking twenty-three-year-old from Canada who was an unemployed former dancer at the notorious Chippendales club. He had been living with a wealthy older woman, but had outstayed his welcome and was looking for shelter. The son of a Jewish mother and Catholic father, Charlie was raised in an Italian-Catholic neighborhood but had warm feelings for his Jewish grandfather. He was estranged from his immediate family and chose me to be his father figure; he changed his name to Mair, his grandfather's Jewish name. We became close, and he gradually took on aspects of Jewish observance, including the wearing of tefillin, the black leather straps and boxes worn by traditional Jewish men at prayer.

Charlie eventually came to be considered my thirteenth child. (My wife and I have five daughters and seven sons, thank God.) One day, he decided to visit his family in Montreal, and insisted he needed to take my tefillin to put on while he was there. While he was there, I later found out, Mair's brother, Mario, walked in on Mair wearing my tefillin. In answer to his brother's many questions, Mair taught his brother how to put on tefillin.

Two weeks later, Mario called me with tragic news: Mair had met up with some old buddies of his, bunged on cocaine, and died. His family did not want anything to do with him, but Mario wanted to give him a proper Jewish burial. I worked with Mario to ensure that Mair was buried according to Jewish law. Mario inherited my tefillin, became observant himself, and now is deeply connected to his Jewish heritage. Mario later told me that he felt Mair's death was not in vain because it was through that tragedy that Mario returned to his Jewish roots.

AVI SHAFRAN

Director of Public Affairs, Agudath Israel of America, New York City

Rabbi Shafran is the spokesman for Agudath Israel, an umbrella organization of ultra-Orthodox congregations. Through his tireless efforts to use the media as a means of explaining Orthodox Judaism and its beliefs, countless people have a better grasp of what it means to be an Orthodox Jew. His most recent book is *Migrant Soul: The Story of an American Ger.*

"And so I have come to recognize how fortunate I am today as well, to be spending my days speaking to fellow Jews, even remotely, from an office in lower Manhattan."

I miss the high school classroom, my first rabbinical vocation. I miss my students, the young men and women with whom I studied Jewish texts, law, and history for nearly two decades. That experience, to me, went to the very core of what being a rabbi is. Because the word "rabbi," so often associated today with sermons, meetings, synagogue management and counseling, implies above all else "teacher." And I was exceedingly fortunate to be able for so long to play that Jewishly essential role, to be a living link in the chain of Jewish educational continuity–to play a part in the intellectual and spiritual development of hundreds of precious young Jews.

I've since moved on to a different sort of rabbinic role: writing for, and representing, a major national Orthodox organization. The man who recruited me for my current position, the late, legendary Rabbi Moshe Sherer, spent much time trying to reassure me that presenting an authentic Jewish perspective on current events through the media–what I spend most of my time doing–is really just the Jewish educational process magnified; that I had essentially expanded, not left, my classroom; that the students were simply older and less immediately visible, but still very much there.

I have to admit that I've never really become fully convinced that my current role is as valuable to the Jewish people as my former one was, though there are certainly times when I can see the wisdom in his words. Although speaking with a reporter or writing an article are hardly the direct human interaction that has sustained the Jewish nation for millennia, in our contemporary geographically far-flung and ideologically multifaceted Jewish world it is certainly a necessary part of helping promote Jewish knowledge and continuity.

And so I have come to recognize how fortunate I am today as well, to be spending my days speaking to fellow Jews, even remotely, from an office in lower Manhattan.

But part of me still pines for the special stimulation of more personal intellectual interaction with others, especially with idealistic minds as yet unset in the stone that so often comes to encase our attitudes over time, minds hungry for the challenge of receiving the Torah anew, of grappling with it, of learning to love and cherish it.

And that's why, whenever, as occasionally occurs, someone approaches me on a train or bus or ferry and opens a conversation with "Rabbi, could you answer a question for me?" I feel especially blessed, and try to respond the best I can.

NACHUM SHIFREN

Author; Surfer

Rabbi Shifren is the author of *Surfing Rabbi: A Kabbalistic Quest for the Soul.*

"I have a lot of satisfaction from learning Torah, and every day I feel like I am finding out something that is very new and awesome and profound. It keeps the fire stoked."

While I was growing up, surfing, to a large degree, was a substitute for my lack of religious identity. I had no connection with my heritage, because my parents were not involved with Judaism at all. But through surfing, I became aware of a power greater than me. I had a spiritual life through surfing–everything felt supernatural while I was riding the waves.

When I got older, I lived in Hawaii and Mexico for about five years each. Surfing was my life. But I was very impressed by my younger brother, who had moved to Israel and fought in the 1973 Yom Kippur War. I had always been influenced very profoundly by the Holocaust, and the victimhood of the Jews then. Around 1977, I decided to follow my brother to Israel, where I, too, joined the army. Because I was in such good shape, I was made a combat fitness instructor. It was important for me at the time to be able to identify Judaism with strength, rather than weakness.

But I still was not interested in Judaism as a religious way of life. At some point, I read a philosophy book that said, "Be who you are." I thought about that and wondered why I was running away from who I was. I was very cynical and did not believe anything said by any rabbi or organized religion. It was difficult for me to connect.

When I was in graduate school at the University of California at Santa Barbara, and it came to be Hanukkah time, I decided I wanted to light candles, because my parents always lit Hanukkah candles. I called the one rabbi in the area, who turned out to be affiliated with Chabad, and he sent me candles. That started a relationship that has lasted twenty years so far. He was a body surfer from Australia, so he and I had a connection through the surf. I started studying Judaism with him, which continued even after I graduated and started teaching in Los Angeles. I would drive to his house every Sabbath. I suddenly wanted to discover what learning Torah was all about. Some people's involvement with Judaism is all about doing various rituals, but I wanted to delve into the reasons why things are what they are. So I

decided to move to Israel once again. I sold all my surfboards, which obviously was difficult for me, and stayed in Israel, during which time I was ordained as a rabbi. At the age of thirty-five, I started to get seriously interested in my heritage, and my quest has gone on until this day.

By the time I got interested in my Jewish heritage, it was not a big transition. A lot of people find it difficult to make the change to an Orthodox lifestyle. But as a surfer, I needed to be very disciplined and dedicated, so the transition to a religious lifestyle of discipline and dedication was not such a problem.

Who knows how things would have turned out differently if I had grown up as an Orthodox Jew? My whole life would have been greatly changed, but I am very glad things worked out as they did. I have a lot of satisfaction from learning Torah, and every day I feel like I am finding out something that is very new and awesome and profound. It keeps the fire stoked.

I have maintained my dual life as a rabbi and surfer, but there is no great divide between these two aspects of my world. When you are a surfer, you are very close to God, very close to the forces of creation. You isolate yourself from society, throw yourself into an ocean that is uninhabitable, and search for the perfect wave–you are trying to tap into the very essence of the forces of creation. Every surfer feels this at some level, even if it is very subliminal for many. Some people feel a deep inner need to be disconnected from their physicality, to go beyond their bodies, and the world of surfing offers just that. When you are racing along on a wave, you feel like you are not part of the earth anymore, and in a way, that is the religious experience, trying to go beyond physical limitations to a more profound level. In that sense, there is a strong sense of connection between surfing and spirituality, a connection that has shaped my life.

TONI SHY

Spiritual Leader of Temple Beth Israel, Port Washington, N.Y.

"Shy! Wait!" Instead of leaving the hospital, I turned around and went back in. Another congregant was ill. It was a friend of the family who had sought me out. It was serious. The enemy was something called Guillain-Barre Syndrome. I had no idea what it was. I would come to know it very well.

Murray was a bright young man, forty, married, with two young sons. I would learn about Murray and about Linda, his wife, and the extraordinary relationship they shared as I accompanied them on a fight against death over the next few days.

Perfectly healthy, Murray woke up one morning with numbness in his legs. An alert doctor ordered him into the hospital, as that numbness was going to move upward, threatening the function of vital organs. When I first saw Murray, he could still speak. "This crazy thing" wasn't yet real. He had been reading some books on spirituality that sparked some fun discussions as we got to know each other in those early hours. But by the next day, the fun stopped. Murray's speech had become labored, and with it the realization that this threat was real. His rapid debilitation had raised questions about mortality and about God. And he was so worried for Linda and his sons.

Soon, Murray was put on a respirator. I had to run through the alphabet to construct the words he so wanted to say. Then Linda became his interpreter. They had always been amazingly attuned to one another, able to read the other's thoughts. Now it became a necessity. And then Murray could no longer communicate. The disease was at a crucial point and Linda was forced to make rapid-fire, life and death decisions. Complications arose at every turn. Everything was a gamble. There were no assurances, certainly not that he would survive. And always on her mind was what to tell her sons. How not to alarm them when every machine in intensive care screamed, "Alarm!"

Spending those hours with Linda and Murray, being permitted to hold them, pray with and for them, and offer whatever support I could as we lived through days of unrelenting tension, was why I became a rabbi. There is no gift more precious than being able to help. The privilege of the cloth is being able to love people unabashedly, even as I share my love of God with them. Linda and Murray are incredibly fine people. Every moment I spent with them enriched my life. And thankfully, there will be many more.

Murray survived his ordeal, and amazingly, had almost no recollection of what happened. It was Linda who was most shaken. Together they reconstructed the events, and eventually Murray returned home to his beautiful boys. Years have passed, and their lives have returned to normal. I know I will never forget the time my life converged with theirs, and I am every mindful, and grateful, that we were able to live happily ever after.

This—and so many stories like it—speaks louder than any explanation I can give for why I am a rabbi and what it means to me.

RONALD SOBEL

Senior Rabbi, Congregation Emanu-El of New York City

"To bring comfort to those who grieve, courage to those who need, hope to those who see themselves hopeless, love to those who feel loveless, these are the challenges that the rabbi meets..."

Nelson Glueck, the world-renowned archaeologist and later president of the Hebrew Union College, placed his hands upon my shoulders, and in so doing, ordained me as a rabbi. Gazing into my eyes with his own penetrating look, he quietly asked if I was prepared to accept the burden of the Torah. That question during that moment, forty years ago, filled me with incomparable awe and profound trepidation. Henceforth, my life was to be as a teacher to the Jewish people. The responsibility was overwhelming, even as the implicit challenge was daunting. Though more confident and significantly more self-assured, four decades later I still feel, everyday, the magnitude of the responsibility.

The challenges confronting the rabbi in modernity are the same, but yet, different from those with which rabbis have had to deal for the better part of the past two millennia. In today's world the rabbi has to validate himself or herself again and again, to prove worthy of the title "my teacher." The possession of rabbinic ordination is only the beginning. The heart of the rabbi must be continuously gentle, the soul forever compassionate, and the intellect always alive and inquiring. Today, the rabbi is not only the teacher of Torah, the rabbi must, by the way he or she lives, become a Torah, an embodiment of what we believe to be that which God expects of us all. Can there be a greater challenge?

To bring comfort to those who grieve, courage to those who need, hope to those who see themselves hopeless, love to those who feel loveless, these are the challenges that the rabbi meets between each rising in the morning and every retiring in the evening. At the same time the teacher of Torah must bring the tradition's wisdom to the problems of the hour. Indeed, daunting are the challenges.

However, there can be no greater joy than that which comes from knowing that some of those challenges have been met successfully.

JACOB STAUB

Vice President for Academic Affairs, Reconstructionist Rabbinical College

Rabbi Staub is co-author of *Exploring Judaism: A Reconstructionist Approach;* author, *The Creation of the World According to Gersonides;* and co-editor, *Creative Jewish Education: A Reconstructionist Approach.*

"RRC's curriculum, in which Judaism was studied as an evolving religious civilization and all beliefs and practices were studied in historical context, offered me the opportunity to relearn what I had tried so unsuccessfully to forget and to reclaim the treasures of the Jewish tradition."

When I told my parents at age twenty that I had decided to become a rabbi, they took offense and told me that I should not joke about such things. Modern Orthodox lifelong members of Young Israel synagogues who had sent their son to Yeshiva Rabbi Israel Salanter, they had suffered my departure from the community during my adolescence. They could not, at that moment, imagine that someone like me could be a rabbi.

My decision to attend the Reconstructionist Rabbinical College was made without ambivalence. I had lost faith in Orthodoxy right before I had become a bar mitzvah. I no longer believed that the Torah was divinely revealed and the mitzvot commanded by God. I had tried very hard to abandon my Jewish identity because I was unaware that there were alternatives to being Orthodox. But I had failed. When I heard the Yiddish or Israel music playing on WEVD, when the Six-Day War broke out, I felt deeply my Jewish connections as something I couldn't seem to shake.

My discovery of the Reconstructionist movement was accidental but immediately life-changing. When I began to read the works of Rabbi Mordecai Kaplan, I was amazed: Here was a man raised by a father who was a prominent Orthodox rabbi. Kaplan had encountered doubts like mine and had found a way to remain devoted to Judaism without abandoning reason and science. I read all of his very thick books.

Back in New York City during an intersession from college, I attended a Shabbat morning service at the Society for the Advancement of Judaism. I remember how emotionally stressful it was to walk into the sanctuary. The morning davvening, in its words and melodies, was extremely similar to the Young Israel service in which I had been raised. I had been inside of a synagogue in the U.S. only a handful of times over the previous seven years. Just hearing the *nusach* (traditional melody) of the service sung upset me thoroughly, bringing back emotionally traumatic memories from my yeshiva experience. And then, Rabbi Alan Miller delivered the *devar torah*, Rabbi Kaplan responded, and congregants joined in the sermon-dialogue. These people were like me. They did not shrink from raising hard questions. They did not believe that the Torah was literally revealed or that *halakhah* (Jewish law) was binding. And yet, they clearly loved it all, and they attended synagogue joyfully participating in prayer. There was an alternative to the Judaism in which I had been raised!

I had been planning at that point to study for a Ph.D. in English literature. I was a serious fiction writer. But soon thereafter I knew that it was Judaism in which I wanted to immerse myself. RRC's curriculum, in which Judaism was studied as an evolving religious civilization and all beliefs and practices were studied in historical context, offered me the opportunity to relearn what I had tried so unsuccessfully to forget and to reclaim the treasures of the Jewish tradition. I went to rabbinical school not because I was sure I wanted to be a rabbi but because I was sure I wanted to learn, and RRC provided an approach in which I could return to Jewish learning.

Twenty years later, I asked my mother how she reconciled her own religious beliefs with the pride she clearly felt about my accomplishments as a Reconstructionist rabbi. She responded that she believed that the Blessed Holy One had chosen me as a *shaliach*, a messenger, to reach out to Jews who had fallen away. While I do not share her faith in *hashgahah peratit*, in God's providential governance of the details of our lives, I do think that she knew me well. My rabbinic career has indeed been motivated by a passion for sharing the riches of Judaism with others.

JOSEPH TELUSHKIN

Author, *Jewish Literacy* and *The Book of Jewish Values*

Author of numerous books on Judaism, such a *Jewish Literacy* and the *Book of Jewish Values,* Rabbi Telushkin is perhaps the best-known and most-influential explainer of traditional Judaism to the masses, both Jewish and non-Jewish.

"Most of my rabbinical work has been done through writing. I have tried to supply modern Jews with basic knowledge that will enable them to be Jewishly literate."

My primary goal as a rabbi and as a writer of books on Judaism is to help restore ethics to their central place in Judaism. It is unfortunate, but religiosity today is often associated exclusively with ritual observance. Thus, if two Jews are speaking about whether or not a certain individual is "religious," the answer will be based entirely on the person's level of religious observance: "He keeps the Sabbath and kashrut, so he is religious" or "He does not keep the Sabbath or kashrut, so he is not religious."

From these types of attitudes, one can form the extraordinarily peculiar impression that in Judaism, ethics are an extracurricular activity. Yet throughout history, when Judaism's greatest teachers were asked to define Judaism's essence, they have done so in ethical terms. The most famous instance is the case of the non-Jew who asked Rabbi Hillel–the first century B.C.E. sage–to define the essence of Judaism while standing on one foot. Hillel answered, "What is hateful to you, do not do unto your neighbor; the rest is commentary. Now go and study." So it is a tragedy–and false to the spirit of Judaism–that ethics have been marginalized.

I make this assertion as a Jew who believes in the great importance of rituals. Without rituals, you cannot achieve a sense of holiness; trying to have a sacred Shabbat experience devoid of ritual is futile. Also, without rituals, there is no mode for transmitting Judaism from generation to generation. Rituals also reinforce ethical teachings. My friend Dennis Prager says that when he was six years old, the first words he learned to read in English were "pure vegetable shortening only," ensuring that he stayed away from anything with animal fat that would therefore be unkosher: In other words, it's not a bad thing to learn at the age of six that you cannot have every candy bar in the candy store.

Some years ago, it occurred to me that the Jewish laws of *lashon hara*–which legislate that we must avoid speaking unfairly about others–have a great deal to teach all Americans, not just Jews. Most Americans, Jews and non-Jews alike, believe, for example, that it is acceptable to transmit even very negative information about another person, as long as the information is true. The Jewish teaching is different. If something is true but negative, you should not say it, unless the person to whom you are speaking needs the information. In truth, it is quite rare that the person to whom you are speaking needs the information, yet most people heedlessly pass on truths and half-truths that can destroy another person's good name.

With this thought in mind, I approached senators Joseph Lieberman and Connie Mack in 1996 to introduce a Senate resolution establishing a National Speak No Evil Day in the United States. As of yet, the resolution has not yet passed, but there is a new effort underway to get such a day declared. I will be very proud if this happens, because the establishment of such a day would be a genuine contribution to the United States, a nation that has been more welcoming to Jews than any other society in which we have ever lived.

Most of my rabbinical work has been done through writing. I have tried to supply modern Jews with basic knowledge that will enable them to be Jewishly literate. And what has been so gratifying is that there are so many Jews who are open to learning about Judaism and the implications of its teachings for their daily lives. To cite one example: Ask even relatively knowledgeable Jews what the word mitzvah means, and the response often will be "good deed." But in reality, mitzvah means "commandment." The difference between the two is subtle but significant. "Good deed" implies a voluntary act, while "commandment" is clearly an obligatory one. Though most of us believe that a voluntary act is on a higher ethical plane than one done out of a sense of obligation, the Talmud–the standard work of Jewish law– takes precisely the opposite point of view: "Greater is he who is commanded and carries out an act than he who is not commanded and carries it out" (Kiddushin 31a).

DAVID TEUTSCH

Director, Center for Jewish Ethics, Reconstructionist Rabbinical College, and Lou and Myra Wiener Professor of Contemporary Jewish Civilization

Rabbi Teutsch was editor-in-chief of the six-volume *Kol Haneshamah* prayer-book series. He is past president of the Reconstructionist Rabbinical College.

"...I have had an opportunity to help strengthen the moral fiber of the movement by helping people connect the things they believe in to how we actually function in our public and communal lives."

I attended college during the Vietnam War era of the early 1970s. At that time, my thoughts of earning a doctorate and becoming a philosophy professor or going to law school and then into politics seemed of questionable value when considered against the backdrop of the social upheaval all around me. I sought solace in the continuity of Jewish tradition and realized in doing so that religious community could provide a basis for the moral work that lay at the heart of what I cared most about. I decided to major in Jewish studies and went to seminary following graduation from Harvard.

I struggled for a long time to find my place in the Jewish community. My first rabbinic position was a small congregation in Rockland County, New York, where my faith in the power of democratic community was tested and, ultimately, deepened. After five years as a congregational rabbi, I served a stint as a senior staff member at what is now called CLAL–the National Jewish Center for Learning and Leadership–where I witnessed the transformative power of adult education. Ultimately, I found my home in the Reconstructionist movement, first as executive director of the Jewish Reconstructionist Federation and subsequently in various positions in the administration of the Reconstructionist Rabbinical College. The Reconstructionist movement provided an atmosphere in which I could pursue the things I cared most about: commitment to building democratic communities, balancing rootedness in Jewish tradition with the innovation required by a rapidly changing world, and reinvigorating Jewish spirituality.

My work as executive director of the Jewish Reconstructionist Federation helped me realize the power of the organizational culture of the synagogue to shape Jewish culture today. To fully understand the implications of that insight I resumed graduate study and earned a doctorate in social systems from the Wharton School of the University of Pennsylvania.

In developing ways to enhance democratic decision-making in congregations and in popularizing values-based decision-making, I have had an opportunity to help strengthen the moral fiber of the movement by helping people connect the things they believe in to how we actually function in our public and communal lives. And I'm grateful as well for the opportunity I have had to serve as editor-in-chief of *Kol Haneshamah*, the groundbreaking Reconstructionist prayer-book series that has provided a powerful tool for spiritual development and Jewish education. It directly applies the social theories about teaching values, strengthening community, and molding shared experience.

As president of the Reconstructionist Rabbinical College for nine years, I focused on helping this graduate and professional school to evolve and develop as a model community. I will be stepping down from the presidency in 2002 in order to devote more time to teaching and scholarship. As the director of the Center for Jewish Ethics at the College, I am developing materials and teaching methods to make it easier for rabbis to carry this approach more broadly across North America. I am deeply grateful that the rabbinate has provided such wonderful opportunities for learning and serving, personal growth, and acting on the basis of passionate commitment.

YITZCHAK (ELIO) TOAFF
Chief Rabbi of Italy

The Chief Rabbi of Italy, Rabbi Toaff is a descendant of important Italian rabbis of yore.

"The chief significance of being a rabbi, to me, is the fundamental duty of being master not only in scholarly matters, but also in life."

When I was rabbi in Ancona, Italy, I was living one hundred meters from the Church of Jesus, where a priest was officiating. I encountered this priest, Don Bernadino, every morning when I was returning to my home at the temple. It was in 1942, and the persecution against the Jews due to the German invasion was becoming stronger.

One morning when I encountered Don Bernardino, he made a sign to me not to go home and to follow him to the priest's quarters. So I went with him, and he advised me that the Germans were in my home and were waiting for me. When the racial laws were issued, I was the rabbi in Ancona and I was truly preoccupied with aiding the escape flight of some young Jews who lived there. I was looking into every way of helping them make an escape to Switzerland, which held the potential for entrance either legally or illegally. But then that option also closed, and I found myself with the youths in grave danger. So I decided to go and talk to the guards of our zone, and they agreed to allow these youths to escape capture. I am able to say with satisfaction that–with no exception–not one of the Jewish youths was denounced or deported.

I was born in Livorno on April, 15, 1915, where I went to the Superior Institute of Hebrew Studies and the Classical Lyceum. I graduated in jurisprudence at the University of Pisa in 1938, and then I followed as a graduate of rabbinical studies in 1939. In 1941, I was appointed to head the Hebrew Community of Ancona, in Venice, and finally in 1951 in Rome. I became a rabbi because I believe firmly in the ideals of this mission.

The chief significance of being a rabbi, to me, is the fundamental duty of being master not only in scholarly matters, but also in life. As chief rabbi, I have had responsibility for the spiritual direction of the community and the efficacy of all the services offered. I decided to resign, though, in late 2001, telling my congregation, "It is time to take my leave of you. I am doing so by my own free choice, and with great emotion. I hope that a young man will take up the reins of this ancient community."

MARVIN TOKAYER

Former Chief Rabbi of Japan; Rabbi, Cherry Lane Minyan, Great Neck, N.Y.

Rabbi Tokayer is rabbi of the Cherry Lane Minyan, an orthodox synagogue in Great Neck, N.Y. He served for many years as rabbi of the Jewish community in Japan and director of religion, educational, and cultural activities for the federation of Jewish communities of southeast Asia and the Far East. He has written twenty-eight books on Jews and Judaism. He is married and has four children and seven grandchildren.

"If anyone in this huge territory was interested in Judaism, Jews, Hebrew, the Bible, Zionism, or anything related to the Jewish civilization, mine was the only telephone number."

I served as a United States Air Force chaplain for two years in the Far East. I would ride a monthly circuit, covering the Air Force, Navy, Coast Guard, and Marine Corps of Japan, Okinawa, Korea, China, Vietnam, Thailand, and Philippines. Subsequently, I was asked by the Jewish Community of Japan to become the rabbi of its Jewish community.

The original suggestion to return to Asia and take the position in Tokyo came from the Lubavitcher Rebbe, even though I am certainly not a Hasid, or one of his followers. When I was a rabbinical student, I wrote a letter to the Rebbe, asking to discuss with him some aspects of Jewish philosophy. He invited me to visit, and we spent about two hours together. Later, when I was engaged to be married, we met again, and he urged us to go to Japan, which caught us by surprise, because we were not at all interested in going to Japan. But he kept making the point that a captain has no right to abandon his outpost. He promised that it would be good for the community, and very good for us as well.

We went, originally planning to stay for two years, and ended up spending more than ten years in Japan. They were the best years of my life. I had a congregation of "talking books"—everyone had an amazing story to tell. I had congregants who had lived in Mongolia, Harbin, Tientsin, Shanghai, and Singapore. Each one could speak volumes concerning the Jewish experience in the Far East. For years, I just listened to them and did not say a word, and I learned so much from them.

The day I arrived in Tokyo, there was a welcome party, to give us an opportunity to meet the community. As I met the first person who arrived, I asked—for some unknown reason—"Where are you from?" He answered, "Mongolia," and I asked what he had been doing there. He told me that he had owned a department store. "But don't worry, rabbi," he said. "It was closed on Shabbos." He proceeded to take out his wallet and show me a photograph of a department store in Mongolia with a Star of David over the main entrance.

Another time, a Japanese man called me from a pay phone soon after my arrival in Tokyo. I had

difficulty understanding him, and I asked whether he spoke any language other than Japanese. He told me he spoke German—and Yiddish. I could hardly believe it. "Shalom aleichem," I said, offering the traditional Yiddish greeting. "Aleichem shalom," he said, accurately, in response. I continued the conversation in Yiddish, and told him to come over immediately. He was self-taught, but had never heard the language; it was all from books. His academic field was German and Kafka; in the literature, Yiddish would sometimes be mentioned, and he did not know what it was. So he taught himself the language but did not know what it was supposed to sound like. We never got to sleep that night. I made a tape for him of Yiddish lullabies and all the popular Yiddish songs. I later helped him secure a grant to study Yiddish at Columbia University and in Israel, where he lived among the Hasidim who speak Yiddish as their first language.

I was the only rabbi in the area: China has over one billion people, India has almost as many, Japan has 120 million people. If anyone in this huge territory was interested in Judaism, Jews, Hebrew, the Bible, Zionism, or anything related to the Jewish civilization, mine was the only telephone number. I knew that everyday somebody would call, though I never knew who it would be or where it would come from. I became a type of ambassador or Jewish representative, building bridges of understanding to the Eastern world. If there was an ecumenical conference in India, and the Buddhists, Hindus, Sikhs, Muslims, and Christians were there, the Jews should also be represented. It was a great challenge, but it was also a great opportunity.

Being a rabbi means being the interpreter and the messenger of the Jewish tradition to the Jewish people. I have never had a bad day in the rabbinate. You need to wear so many hats: the rabbi, the teacher, the preacher, the fundraiser, the counselor, the scholar. It is impossible to do all that. Nevertheless, I have such a healthy respect for Jewish tradition and civilization; for me to be the representative and teacher of this tradition to our people gives me the greatest self-satisfaction.

THEODORE TSURUOKA

Spiritual Leader, Temple Isaiah, Great Neck, N.Y.

Theodore Tsuruoka is a second-genera-tion Japanese American and an early convert to Judaism. After suc-cessful careers in both the public and private sectors, he has discovered his life's calling. Though not yet a rabbi–he is nearing completion of his ordination studies at the Academy for Jewish Religion– he serves as spiritual leader of Temple Isaiah of Great Neck, N.Y.

"I was thoroughly taken in by the Torah....It became a passion of mine to introduce the Torah to others so that they, too, might be ignited by its words."

My life has been a journey from my earli-est childhood recollections of growing up on the Upper West Side of New York until this very moment. It has been a spiritual journey taking me from the Japanese-American Methodist Church–which met in a brownstone at Riverside Drive and 108th Street–to the pulpit of a Reform Jewish temple in Great Neck, New York, where I serve as the rabbi. Throughout my journey of nearly half a century, I have felt that God was with me as a gentle guide, opening doors to new worlds, and closing some doors of past life experiences. My relationship with God has changed over these years, but my sense of God's nearness has remained steadfast.

Conversion to Judaism was a major event in my life. It has made it possible for me to be close to God in ways I felt I could never have experi-enced previously. Becoming Jewish meant joining a community of faith, adopting the history of an ancient people, praying in a common language, and aiming to make every daily act an expression of sacredness.

The Jewish community is the strength of our people. My journey brought our family to Temple Emanuel in Lynbrook, New York, located on the South Shore of suburban Long Island. We had originally joined for the purpose of securing a Jewish education for our two children, Jeffrey and Amy. The congregation was very welcoming and did everything it could to make us feel at home and part of the community. It did not take long for both Linda and I to become active members of the congregation.

It was there that I met a rabbi who made possible for me something that had been but a dream up to that time. A few weeks after the end of the High Holy Days, Rabbi Stuart Geller asked me if I would be interested in chanting the Torah portion for the following Rosh Hashanah. This would mean learning how to read directly from the Torah and learning to chant the verses accord-ing to a strict set of melodies. With nearly a year to prepare, I agreed to his offer.

For the next few months, Rabbi Geller would call me on Saturday mornings, two hours before services, and ask me to meet him in the sanctuary, so that I could practice the Torah portion. Through gentle suggestions and by patient example, he taught me how to chant from the Torah. Along the way, he showed me a depth of faith and love of Torah that still drives me. We would carefully remove the Torah's silver crowns, yad (pointer), and breastplate, and then take off the beautifully embroidered mantle from the sacred scroll. We would unroll the scroll and examine the panels. Sometimes we would pause on some section, dis-cuss a special letter, or examine how the words were laid out on the parchment. He told me how a scribe–long gone, a victim of the Holocaust– lovingly and carefully wrote each letter with full attention to detail, completely focused on his holy task.

Rabbi Geller showed me how to look for God in the Torah. He showed me how the Torah can be a means for a two-way conversation with the Divine. I was thoroughly taken in by the Torah. Soon I was helping our b'nei mitzvah children mas-ter their Torah and Haftarah portions. It became a passion of mine to introduce the Torah to others so that they, too, might be ignited by its words.

My synagogue involvement reached its peak when I became president of the Temple. This expe-rience has been helpful to me in understanding what it takes to create good working relationships between the clergy and the congregation. Soon after, I decided to leave my family business and enter rabbinical school at the Academy for Jewish Religion. My love of Torah that so deepened under Rabbi Geller's guidance made this a clear choice. In my role as spiritual leader of my own synagogue in Great Neck, it is my goal to give back to my community something of what I have received from others during my spiritual journey: a love for Torah and a sense of pride in being Jewish.

Looking back on my family history, it might seem amazing that I have arrived at the place I am today. My grandparents immigrated from Japan at the beginning of the last century and were detained in an internment camp during W.W. II. But here I am. It has been a wonderful journey. And I thank God every day for sustaining me.

ARTHUR WASKOW

Director, The Shalom Center; activist for *tikkun olam*
(spiritually rooted action to heal the world)

Rabbi Waskow
is the author of
*Godwrestling–
Round 2*; *Down-to-
Earth Judaism*; and
Seasons of Our Joy;
and co-author of
*A Time for Every
Purpose Under
Heaven*: *The Jewish
Life-Spiral as a
Spiritual Path*. In
1996 he was named
a Wisdom-Keeper
by the U.N., in
connection with the
Habitat II confer-
ence in Istanbul.

*"I could feel Passover
erupting on the
streets, and the streets
erupting on my
dinner table and
inside myself. I had
no idea this energy
was inside me, but
I was struck by it."*

I became bar mitzvah in an Orthodox synagogue, though my parents were not observant. In our Baltimore neighborhood in the 1930s, communal life centered around that synagogue. My bar mitzvah celebration was absolutely a boilerplate affair: I was taught to chant the Torah without being taught any meaning of the text. The event could have been incredibly rich and full of meaning, but it was not dealt with that way at all. I just went through the motions, and soon lost all my involvement in Judaism. I didn't get reinvolved in any serious way until 1968, when I was thirty-four.

The transformative event for me came during the spring of 1968. I had been strongly involved as an activist, teacher, and public intellectual around issues of nuclear disarmament, the Vietnam War, Civil Rights, and racism. I worked at the Institute for Policy Studies, an independent think tank in Washington. On April 4, 1968, Martin Luther King Jr. was murdered, and the next day, the black community of Washington, D.C., erupted. There was, essentially, an uprising, and Pres. Lyndon Johnson sent the army in, put the city under military occupation, and imposed a curfew. Thousands of African-Americans were arrested under the curfew, while whites who were on the streets were ignored. I devoted myself to getting food, medical supplies, doctors, and lawyers from the white suburbs to the black community.

Ten days after the assassination, Passover came. The seder was the only Jewish ritual that I continued to practice; it had powerful echoes from my childhood and was a celebration of freedom, which accorded with my values. On the afternoon before the seder, as I walked home to prepare for it, I passed detachments of the U.S. Army. A jeep with a machine gun was pointing at my block, and this brought from deep inside me the overwhelming sense that this was Pharaoh's army.

All the echoes of my involvement in the Civil Rights movement–the songs built on Exodus, Dr. King's last speech, which deliberately echoed Moses–came rushing forward. For the first time, we stopped in the middle of the seder to weave what was happening at the seder with what was happening on the street. The seder narrative says that in every generation, we must feel as if we ourselves came out of slavery. I could feel Passover erupting on the streets, and the streets erupting on my dinner table and inside myself. I had no idea this energy was inside me, but I was struck by it.

By the fall, I found myself sitting with my Haggadah on one knee and passages from Dr. King, Thoreau, and other sources on the other knee, weaving all these together. I came out with something very different from the traditional Haggadah, which at first I thought I would just use privately with my family. But I found myself calling up friends and colleagues to read them portions of it, so word got around that I was creating a radical version of the Passover Haggadah.

Then, a group in Washington called Jews for Urban Justice asked to use the new Haggadah to do a Freedom Seder on the first anniversary of Dr. King's death, which was the third night of Passover in 1969. It took place in the basement of a black church in Washington, and 800 people came. It was carried live on radio and broadcast on Canadian television a couple days later, and I realized there were thousands of Jews who responded the same way I did to the historic events of the time. I found myself drawn into what I would now call Jewish Renewal, though we did not know what to call it then.

I wasn't ordained until 1995. I had felt really good about being a non-rabbi who was unearthing a Judaism that really mattered to people. Then I began to feel more and more connected to the rabbinic revolution of 2,000 years ago, which responded to cataclysmic changes in the ancient world by transforming–and thereby saving–Judaism. Ordination did not signal a radical break in what I was doing. Since then, I have done a greater amount of overseeing lifecycle ceremonies and transformations. I have gone on teaching and writing. But it has felt within me like that deep identification as a rabbi really made a difference in my own *neshama* (soul), my own sense of values, my own sense of how to see the world.

PETER WEINTRAUB

President, Bristol Associates, Ltd.; teacher, Union of American Hebrew Congregations

For twenty years, Rabbi Weintraub, an ordained Reform Rabbi and full-time international businessman, has made outreach the cornerstone of his life. Through the introduction to Judaism program at the Union of Hebrew Congregations, he has led thousands into Judaism as proud and committed Jews by choice, creating a strong foundation for the future of Judaism's dynamic faith.

"I am not what they have in mind when they think of a Rabbi, and this initial challenge to their preconceptions prepares them to rethink other stereotypes and misconceptions about Judaism."

It is early in the morning, and my day is already in full swing. I sit in my office, surrounded by desks and tables. To my right sit a stack of books and notes from last night's class in Midrash. The debate centered around Moses and his impact on world culture. One of my students, who only recently discovered he is Jewish, engaged in discussion with another, a non-Jew planning to convert. At 10:30 P.M., everyone reluctantly agreed to break until the following week.

Rabbi/Businessman. That is my title, what I tell people I am when they ask. Those who know me primarily as a businessman are often not surprised to hear that I also am a rabbi. They say they can sense that I approach business in a different way. That I seem to have a balance, a sense of perspective, that is rare in the business world.

My students feel the same way. Most of them come from the business world themselves, and all come from secular backgrounds. They come to my introduction to Judaism class–which I have taught for many years at Union of American Hebrew Congregations–curious but wary. I am not what they have in mind when they think of a Rabbi, and this initial challenge to their preconceptions prepares them to rethink other stereotypes and misconceptions about Judaism. The religion I introduce them to is designed to enrich lives that are lived fully in the world. I am an example to them that there is no inherent conflict between spirituality and commerce. On the contrary: each gives relevance to the other.

I always try to mix religion and business. Indeed, each world has so blended with the other that I rarely spend a day in only one. When I travel to Los Angeles, I meet with Hassan Hassan, a Palestinian-American client. As we sit over tea in his home, the discussion invariably turns to Jerusalem. He yearns to return to his home in Tourmas Aya, but the deteriorating situation there makes that dream all but impossible. We sip tea and decide that if we were in power, there would be peace between our peoples. A delusion, certainly. We are neither politicians nor world leaders. And

yet, as we sit doing business, a Palestinian and a rabbi acting in mutual self-interest and respect, the question arises: We may be the exception, but can real peace be built from any less?

Back home, my phone messages testify to my mixed vocation. A few are from customers inquiring about their shipments or eager to place orders for the coming season.

One is from my son David, the third of five children my wife, Ellen, and I have been blessed with. He is spending the year in Israel, his commitment to his work/study fellowship stronger than his fear of terrorism. Today, he has more prosaic concerns: what type of furniture to buy for his room in the house he shares with three Israelis.

A representative from a rabbinical organization, the Central Conference of American Rabbis, calls, asking me to represent Reform Judaism at a conference of rabbis from across the denominational spectrum. We will meet to try and find common ground, to minimize the fraternal squabbles that weaken our people at a time when we need, more than ever, to be strong.

Three Pakistani suppliers want to know if I can still travel to Pakistan after the tragedy of September 11. Perhaps, they suggest, it would be better for them to come to New York.

And the final call is from the director of the Union of Hebrew Congregations, to discuss the funeral plans for Debbie, a former student who perished in the World Trade Center on September 11. Two years earlier I officiated at her wedding, and now I will be saying the mourner's Kaddish at her funeral–a prayer in praise of a God whose will sometimes defies comprehension.

When I was a young rabbi contemplating entering business, I was encouraged by the example of the great French Rabbi, Rashi, who also ran a vineyard. Rashi's deceptively simple style never fails to penetrate straight to the heart of the matter. I like to think that at his Sabbath table, Rashi took a special satisfaction at producing his own wine. If so, I understand the sentiment. After nineteen years, I still love the idea, as a man of the cloth, of importing the cloth myself.

SIMKHA WEINTRAUB

Rabbinic Director, New York Jewish Healing Center/Jewish Board
of Family and Children's Services

What is the major challenge I face in my work? First I'll tell you what it isn't. People generally assume that the greatest challenge in my work is the difficulty in dealing, for much of the day, with people facing illness, death, and bereavement. They wonder how one survives the constant drain of the powerful nexus of emotions–loss, disappointment, emptiness, fear, rage, despair, and so on.

Truth be told, these aspects of my work are difficult indeed. It is hard, maybe impossible, not to feel and react to people experiencing such profound pain and suffering–and also, generally, it is insensitive and unhelpful to act detached and unaffected. To be sure, then, it is a daily challenge to be present but not overcome, engaged but not overwhelmed.

But that challenge is reflected in the very people who are coming for help, who need both to groan and to transcend, to bottom-out and rebuild. We are, in the end, simply partners on the journey of the human condition. And on that journey, the Jewish tradition and the Jewish community are great resources in trying to cope and to hope, to survive and to grow.

You know what else is *not* the major challenge? The human condition. The Talmud (Eruvin 13b) describes a protracted debate between the School of Shammai and the School of Hillel concerning a provocative, if theoretical, question: Which would have been better–for humanity not to have been created, or for humanity to have been created? The School of Shammai asserted that it would have been better for humans *not* to have been created at all–a logical, if also depressing, position that, to my mind at least, responds to the suffering that so many people endure.

After some two-and-a-half years of dispute, the Talmudic academy took a vote and decided that Shammai was right–it would have been better had humans *not* been created. But the Talmud appends a kind of disclaimer: "…But now that humans have been created, let them investigate their past deeds, or, as others say, let them examine their future actions." In other words, the problem is not the human condition, which is unchangeable, but what we do in light of that, in response to our reality–which is, at least much of the time, heavily in our influence.

So now let me tell you what the major challenge is: society. It is our society's aversion to facing and integrating illness and disease, its insistence on everyone being young, virile, Ken and Barbie, increasingly and intensely productive, unscarred, ungrieved, and pulled up solely by their own bootstraps. It is the medical and insurance systems that reduce people to objects, that prevent health care professionals from fully relating to and helping people, and do not address the whole person, in all his or her dimensions.

When it comes to loss and bereavement, here, too, the major challenge is the society in which we live, which either cannot handle death and grief at all, or at least wants the survivors to move quickly to a highly functioning, visibly whole and happy mode. People are not only expected back at work within days, they are to do so with no evidence of having approached the abyss or experienced the unraveling of their world.

So then people want to know: what helps you cope with all the tragedy, loss, and despair? It may seem trite to say it, but since September 11 we have been sustained by the remarkable deeds that have reached across ethnic differences, social turflines, and geographic distances. One example: the dozen or so ninety-year-old residents of the Jewish Home for the Aging in L.A., who crocheted beautiful afghans to give to Jews who lost family members in the World Trade Center attacks. When these arrived at our office, a day before a support group of Jewish survivors of the tragedy, we froze, standing in awe of these sacred blankets.

It was only the day after distributing some of these to their intended recipients that I allowed myself to stroke and hug these blankets. Their warmth is both visceral and other-worldly. I am so lucky to be encompassed by these blankets, so honored to pass them on. There really is an eternal Jewish community and a potent Jewish tradition. May these envelop all those who suffer and grieve.

AVI (AVRAHAM) WEISS

Senior Rabbi of the Hebrew Institute of Riverdale; founder and dean of the newly established Modern Orthodox rabbinical school, Yeshivat Chovevei Torah, N.Y.

Until recently, Rabbi Weiss was a full-time faculty member in the Judaic Studies department at Stern College Yeshiva University and the National President of the Coalition for Jewish Concerns-Amcha, a grassroots activist organization.

"My hope for all those I touch is that I may be worthy of enabling them to feel the deep love I have for them, and that I may in some way help them to grow spiritually."

My rabbinical vision is perhaps best reflected in the institutions with which I have been privileged to be involved. The Hebrew Institute of Riverdale (HIR), a synagogue that has grown to more than 800 families in the over quarter-century I've had the honor of serving it, has as its motto: Torah, Outreach, Activism, Israel. First and foremost, I see myself as a teacher with a passion for conveying both the written and oral Torah. Beyond the rigor and stimulation of classrooms and lecture halls, however, Torah also imbues and enriches all aspects of life. Torah defines what we call Outreach, the encounter among Jews of every affiliation seeking a connection to their religion and heritage. Torah inspires Activism, the value of raising a voice of moral conscience through nonviolent protest and demonstrations, which is a linchpin of my rabbinate. And Torah empowers our commitment to Israel—to viewing Israel as a unique historic opportunity with deep religious meaning.

This just gives a glimpse into the HIR; it does not come close to covering the entire picture. The HIR also runs programs for the disabled and the elderly. It is seen as the primary address of women's prayer groups and is at the forefront of interdenominational dialogue in the Riverdale community. All of these activities have their source in Torah and are guided and energized by its principles.

Yeshivat Chovevei Torah, the newly established yeshiva and rabbinical school founded in 1999, also reflects these ideas. The mission of this endeavor, which in just a few short years has succeeded beyond all expectations, includes "the promotion of Ahavat Yisrael in the relationship to all Jews and of respectful interaction of all Jewish movements. …Expanding the role of women in religious life and leadership. …Recognizing our responsibility to improve the world and our capacity to be enriched by it. …Integrating spirituality and God-consciousness into all learning and into all worldly pursuits."

Underlying every program and institution with which I've been associated is the Torah-driven concept of Ahavat Yisrael, the idea that every Jew, regardless of background or affiliation, is a member of the family and deserves our dedication, love, and respect. This notion of Ahavat Yisrael is grounded in the broader idea of Tselem Elokim, the conviction that every human being is created in the image of God. Each and every person on this earth has a holy spark of the divine within his or her soul. Thus, I view my rabbinate as a profound commitment to my inner family, the Jewish people, and, at the same time, a strong dedication to the larger community of humanity. I've always maintained that an enlightened sense of national identity, rather than being a contradiction to universal consciousness, is in fact a prerequisite for it.

My hope for all those I touch is that I may be worthy of enabling them to feel the deep love I have for them, and that I may in some way help them to grow spiritually. One of my favorite stories reflects this yearning. There was once a rebbe who asked his students the following question: "There's a ladder with fifty rungs. One person is on the forty-seventh, the other on the twenty-fifth. Who is higher?" "Of course," his students responded, "the one on the forty-seventh." "No, my children," the rebbe said. "It depends on which way you're going."

DAVID WOLPE

Sinai Temple, Los Angeles

Rabbi Wolpe is the author of five books, including *The Healer of Shattered Hearts: A Jewish View of God and Making Loss Matter: Creating Meaning in Difficult Times.* His synagogue is nationally known for its popular Friday Night Live services.

"I did not know the woman, and immediately I felt like a fraud. Who was I to take in my hands the responsibility for this soul? She was unknown to me in life, and now on the edge of death was I to play such a pivotal role in her declaration of faith in eternity?"

L ike many rabbis, I recall the first time I was called to a deathbed. I felt unworthy. This is how I learned that I was right.

Many Jews are not aware that the rituals of Judaism include a deathbed confessional. It is called the *vidui* (pronounced vee-doo-ee). There are two versions, one to be said by the person who is dying, and one to recited on his or her behalf by a rabbi.

The vidui prays for the recovery of the person who is ill, but goes on to say that if the one who is in imminent danger of death should not recover, the confessional seeks atonement for the sins he committed.

The vidui does not end there. It is a form of *tsiduk hadin*–justification of the Divine judgment. At critical moments in life, Judaism asks that we affirm that, ultimately, God is good. We may not understand, we may be angry, bewildered, hurt, but God is good. When one hears of a death, one should recite the formula "*Baruch Dayan Emeth*"–"Blessed be the righteous judge." Even on the deathbed, this prayer is intended to assuage the fear of dying. God is good in life, and will be merciful beyond.

The vidui contains the central affirmations of Jewish faith: First the *shema*–that God is one. Then the affirmation that God's name (that is, God's manifestation that we can understand) be blessed, and finally, the declaration that the Lord is God. All of this is a way of crying out to the heavens and the earth that we do believe, that in the face of death we do not shrink from the certainty of ultimate redemption.

I was called in to the deathbed of a woman in my congregation. Like most Jews, her family had no idea that there was such a thing as a vidui. They simply let me know she was dying and assumed that I would do what rabbis do, whatever that might be. "Say a prayer for her," they said. I explained the vidui. That was fine, they told me, and they left me alone with her.

I did not know the woman, and immediately I felt like a fraud. Who was I to take in my hands the responsibility for this soul? She was unknown to me in life, and now on the edge of death was I to play such a pivotal role in her declaration of faith in eternity?

I felt grateful that she was not aware of her surroundings. Perhaps she would not know quite how uncomfortable and uncertain I felt. I held her hand. I began to recite the words of the vidui. The power of the words vied with my unease. I read through to the end. I had done my task.

When I returned home that night, I told my wife what had happened. "Who am I," I asked, "to be doing this?" I felt unworthy.

"You are right," she said. "You are unworthy. But you are not doing it. It is being done through you."

In that exchange was the secret of the rabbinate. As long as it was being done by me, as long as I was the source and not the prism, I could not bear it. Everything inside me would get in the way. But I was not the source–like everyone else, I did not deserve to be. I was the instrument, the tradition, and God, used me to bring the vidui to a dying Jew.

The best things we do in life are not the things we do, but the things that are done through us. God, as a last century rabbi once said, speaks the language of human beings. Our actions are God's sentences, our life patterns God's syntax. As Abraham Joshua Heschel wrote, "God speaks slowly in our lives, a syllable at a time, and only at the end of life can we read the sentence backward."

ERIC YOFFIE

President, Union of American Hebrew Congregations

As president of the Reform movement's Union of American Hebrew Congregations, Rabbi Yoffie has taken a very public role in bringing a voice of conscience to public affairs, raising gun control, and other political issues to the level of religious imperative

"The dry bones of American Judaism are stirring. The sparks are visible to all, ready to leap into flame. I became a rabbi because I wanted to tend these flickering sparks so that they might become a roaring fire, lighting the way of the Jewish people and providing warmth and comfort to the world."

I became a rabbi to serve God, study Torah, and repair the fractures of a broken world. All Jews do these things, of course, but—sometimes—rabbis do them a bit more passionately and insistently, and without the distractions that burden others.

I became a rabbi because I am worried. I am worried about the increasing loneliness of modern life, where family and community are sometimes replaced by technology. I am worried that all the devices that make our lives so much easier and faster—the fax, the modem, the cellular phone—also take away our capacity for human connectedness. I am worried that amidst the relentless acceleration of modern life, our soul is lost within us, drowned out by the noise of the world, and by the insistent rumbling of our own insecurities and fear. I am worried that our proud individualism conceals a hunger for belonging and a craving for community and purpose.

I became a rabbi because I am convinced that Judaism has answers to what worries me and to what troubles modern man and woman. We Jews are heirs to one of the great traditions of faith and community and individual righteousness that the world has ever known. Ever since Sinai, Judaism has been about not being alone; it has been about communion with God and finding our way home. Having known God at the mountain, we know what it is to build a community that lives in God's presence.

I became a rabbi because I want to work with and teach a new generation of Jews that is asking all the right questions. These Jews, who feel the finitude and fragility of the human condition, are looking for a Judaism that will speak to their hearts and souls and *kishkes*. Somehow, beneath the surface, they sense the touch of *Shechinah*—the Divine presence—and they are open more than they have ever been to experiences of Jewish worship and Jewish study. They are Jews who are searching for the poetry of faith. They are Jews who want to believe. They are Jews who want to create a Jewish life of purposefulness and historical depth. But they have no idea how to proceed, and I want to help them.

I am aware, of course, of all the crises of Jewish existence: the apathy, the assimilation, the intermarriage. But I believe that Judaism will do what it has done so many times before in times of crisis. It will remain young and creative and revolutionary; it will look inward and discover new modes of spirituality within itself. In short, it will respond to crisis with renewal, and not with denial or despair. But these things happen only when its rabbis are forward-looking, unbending in their faith, and optimistic to the core. And that is what I try very hard to be.

The dry bones of American Judaism are stirring. The sparks are visible to all, ready to leap into flame. I became a rabbi because I wanted to tend these flickering sparks so that they might become a roaring fire, lighting the way of the Jewish people and providing warmth and comfort to the world. Twenty-seven years later, the task is far from done, but I am still excited by the challenge and filled with buoyancy and hope. I have not regretted my decision for a single day.

YITZHAK PESACH ZINGER

Congregation Boneh Y'rushalayim

Rabbi Zinger is
Lt. Colonel in the
Israel Police Force.

*"Israel's police rabbis
provide counseling
for personal
problems arising
at home, which
indicates the trust
and confidence
of police officers
toward these rabbis."*

I have been a rabbi in Israel's police force since soon after my ordination in 1980. The duties of a police rabbi differ from those of a civilian rabbi or a military rabbi. Each rabbi in the police is in charge of a specific region, where he is responsible for all religious matters, including marital counseling for police officers and their families, burial of officers, and of course, teaching and organizing religious ceremonies.

Since 1993, I have been the assistant chief rabbi to the Israeli police. In this role, I serve as the rabbi for the National Police Headquarters (located in Jerusalem), and I also am responsible for purchasing religious items for the entire Israeli police force: mezuzas for offices, all religious items used in Police Department synagogues, Hannukah menorahs, and items for Sabbath observance used by Orthodox police officers.

I was born in Hungary and educated in Hassidic yeshivahs, including the Belz yeshivah. It is a known fact that most police officers are not Orthodox. But everyone in the police force treats police rabbis with the utmost respect. The honor accorded by police men and women to a rabbi is special, especially among the Sephardic police officers, those whose families originated in the Middle East or Mediterranean countries. There are many police officers–mainly Sephardic Jews– whose custom it is to kiss the hand of the rabbi.

During all the years of my service in the Israel Police, it never once happened that anyone belittled my requests, even those at the highest echelons of command in the Police Department. Israel's police rabbis provide counseling for personal problems arising at home, which indicates the trust and confidence of police officers toward these rabbis. This gives me great satisfaction in the course of my everyday work and is a sign of hope for the future of our people.

One of my most memorable experiences was officiating at the wedding of a policeman who had converted to Judaism from Islam. The wedding took place at a Jerusalem synagogue, and the majority of attendees were Arabs from the groom's family who wore their traditional head covering (*kafiyah*).

I recently officiated at a marriage ceremony for the daughter of a policeman. Although there were many prominent rabbis present from the policeman's family, he preferred that a police rabbi officiate, instead of inviting his prominent relatives to do so. This indicates the closeness and warm relationship that police officers feel toward police rabbis. It is that relationship that keeps me doing what I do every day, and makes me proud to be a rabbi in the Israel Police Force.

DEBORAH ZECHER
Hevreh of Southern Berkshire, Great Barrington, Mass.

Rabbi Deborah Zecher serves as rabbi of Hevreh of Southern Berkshire in Great Barrington, Mass. She is grateful to share her life with her husband, Rabbi Dennis Ross and their three children.

"My work as a congregational rabbi presents me with the possibility of integrating all the different parts of who I am."

I first thought about becoming a rabbi soon after my bat mitzvah, which had been exactly what a bat mitzvah should be: a transformative experience, when I felt completely whole and in sync with myself, no small feat for a teenage girl. I somehow knew that being on that *bima* contributed to that feeling, and I eventually realized becoming a rabbi might be the best way to maintain that sense of wholeness and connection. I couldn't have articulated that feeling back then; I just knew I was extraordinarily happy.

That was in 1968, before there were any women rabbis. For me, the desire to be a rabbi was not any sort of political statement, it was simply what I needed to do with my life. It never dawned on me that being a woman might be an obstacle to becoming a rabbi, which in retrospect seems so peculiar and rather naive. As a girl in the late 1960s, I felt that if I put my mind to something, I should be able to do it. Nine years later when I was ready to apply to rabbinical school, Hebrew Union College had already ordained Sally Priesand and a few other women. In 1982, I was the forty-ninth woman ordained.

My first position after ordination was as assistant rabbi at Westchester Reform Temple in Scarsdale, N.Y. My senior rabbi, Rabbi Jack Stern became—and remains—a very important part of my life, as mentor and friend, and now my congregant in my present congregation. The congregation's leaders did not make a big fuss about hiring me, nor was any dissent tolerated on the decision to hire a woman. One member was irritated that the congregation had hired a woman; when he expressed his dissatisfaction to the senior rabbi, he was told, "Maybe this is not the congregation for you." That set the tone: I was a rabbi of the congregation, and that is how I was treated.

My husband, Dennis Ross, is also a rabbi. After leaving New York, we spent several years in Washington, D.C., before moving to the Berkshires, where we remain today. When we arrived here, Hevreh was a congregation of sixty families. I soon discovered that wonderful chemistry that can exist between rabbi and congregation. We currently number almost 400 families as members, and while we occupied a renovated house as our first home for several years, in 1999, we moved into a brand-new space, the first synagogue ever built in our part of the county. I feel privileged to help in the development of our community with a wonderful, creative, and dynamic group of people.

My sister, Elaine, is also a rabbi. People often ask us if our father—or even better, mother—was a rabbi. My response always is, "We've created a dynasty in one generation, between my husband, my sister, and myself." It is a special privilege to have a sister who is a rabbi. Her work in a large, urban congregation and mine in a medium-size almost rural congregation demand different skills and emphases, yet our shared passion for the Jewish community and especially the transforming potential of liturgy and worship unites us in a very powerful way.

My work as a congregational rabbi presents me with the possibility of integrating all the different parts of who and what I am. That sense of connection to the past and future as well as the challenge of giving voice to liberal Jewish tradition and life affirms the happiness I feel for what I do. I believe that finding joy is a crucial component of Jewish life; joyfulness can be an important byproduct of finding meaning and wholeness in our lives. Judaism invites us to celebrate life, and those are not empty words to me.

Occasionally, I am teased about looking so happy during services. On Shabbat and many times during the week, I look out into the congregation and I see people who do not have to be in synagogue, people who make the choice to be Jewish and live Jewish at a time when Jewish identity is an affirmation, not an obligation.

One of the special gifts of the last few years has been the opportunity to serve as mentor to a number of rabbinical students and newly ordained rabbis; the experience of articulating the meaning and lessons of my rabbinate thus far has enriched my life immeasurably. After twenty years as a rabbi, I now know that the anticipation of becoming a rabbi paled in comparison to the reality; the reality is a thousand times better!

OVERLEAF: *Deborah Zecher (left) with her sister Elaine Zecher (right)*

ELAINE ZECHER
Temple Israel, Boston

Rabbi Elaine Zecher is Chair of the Liturgy Committee, Central Conference of American Rabbis. She lives in Newton, Mass., with her husband and three children.

"My idea of the rabbinate was transformed by the community we are in and by the call to respond to our neighbors."

I knew from a young age that I wanted to work in the Jewish community, either in social work or Jewish communal work. But then my sister, six years older than me, entered rabbinical school, and that possibility became accessible. I also had some wonderful teachers and mentors who encouraged me to go into the rabbinate. It was the best decision I ever made, because the rabbinate provides the full spectrum of involvement in the Jewish community: the teaching, the programming, the counseling.

In rabbinical school, I said I would never, ever become a congregational rabbi. But, as a rabbi not working in a congregation, I realized the pulse of Jewish life really was in the synagogue. And so twelve years ago, I came to Temple Israel of Boston, a large community, that was open to what I call "entrepreneurial programming"– coming up with creative ideas and implementing them, ideas from which you do not make money, but you make souls.

My sister and I went into the rabbinate from different perspectives. She went into the rabbinate wanting to work in a synagogue, and I was more interested in the organizational structure. My sister is a great rabbi, and has been beloved by every congregation she has been connected to. That is a great model to have in pursuing a career. People always ask whether our father is a rabbi, and though he is not, it is still something of a family business. We have a brother in between us in age who is Orthodox in his practice; we say someone needs to be the congregant.

We grew up in a small town outside of Pittsburgh. We were a minority in the community. My best friends were all born-again Christians. My decision to become a rabbi came out of that context, along with my youth group, which I loved, Reform Jewish camps, and a home in which Judaism was woven into the very fabric of our being. My parents loved being Jewish, and we felt that. We kept kosher and had Shabbat dinner every week. My parents helped start the synagogue, and my father ran the Jewish newspaper in Pittsburgh. It came very easily to all of us.

I went on to Brandeis University, and then to Hebrew Union College, where I was ordained. I then became the program director at a Jewish Community Center in Stoughton, Mass., and am now entering my twelfth year here at Temple Israel in Boston. It is a very heterogeneous community: 1,500 families, the largest congregation in New England. We are an urban congregation, so our population is quite diverse, and involves a wide range of members.

Our synagogue is located in the Harvard Medical School neighborhood. All of our neighbors are hospitals; we are not a neighborhood synagogue in the traditional sense. I had never been involved in the pastoral side of being a rabbi. I had been immersed in planning conventions and organizing programs, and it really struck me that there was this whole other area of the rabbinate. My idea of the rabbinate was transformed by the community we are in and by the call to respond to our neighbors.

When I was in rabbinical school, I had a dear friend who was hit by a car. What struck me about that experience was how her inner strength was so profound; I met her soul in a way I had never met anybody's soul. I always carried that with me. When I came to Temple Israel, I really began this whole odyssey of work on the soul and thinking about how you nourish the soul even if the body is not well, and how can the soul be healthy even if the body is not. We were one of the first congregations to offer healing services. That was a turn in my rabbinate I never would have anticipated, but it has given me some of the greatest meaning and significance for what I do.

The verse that adorns my *tallis*–prayer shawl– is from Psalm 100 which says, "Worship God in gladness, come before God with joyful singing." Rejoicing is a fundamental part of my rabbinate and experience of Judaism. I firmly believe that living a Jewish life fills us with this joy. It doesn't mean we shouldn't be serious and intense. Rather, we need to find the expressions of joy in our tradition and weave them into the fabric of our lives.